YOUR HUNDRED BEST TUNES

YOUR HUNDRED
BEST TUNES

Alan Keith

J. M. Dent & Sons Ltd · London

Made in Great Britain
at the
Aldine Press · Letchworth · Herts
for
J. M. Dent & Sons Ltd
Aldine House · 26 Albemarle Street · London

This book is set in 11 on 12pt Garamond 156

ISBN 0 460 04214 9

To Pearl, Linda and Brian

CONTENTS

ACKNOWLEDGMENTS

I am particularly indebted to my friends in the BBC gramophone record library who have been ever helpful in the preparation of my programmes. I take this opportunity to thank them for their unfailing kindness.

I wish also to express my gratitude to those in the BBC reference library who, over the years, have assisted me in my search for 'stories' about the music I play, some of which have been incorporated in this book.

My thanks, too, to the Decca Record Company for their valuable co-operation.

PRELUDE

It all began in November 1959 when I dared to stick out my neck and nominate my hundred 'best' tunes. These were to form the basis of the first series of my radio programme of the same name.

Any list of 'best' tunes is bound to be both arbitrary and personal. No two people anywhere are likely to be of the same opinion, as listeners soon made clear when they readily accepted the challenge to compare their lists with mine.

The choosing of best tunes became a favourite parlour game. Not only was the family circle enthusiastic, but there was also an immediate response from such varied sources as Her Majesty's prisons, hospital staff of all kinds and even ships at sea. Lists came in from factories, offices, schools and service personnel at home and abroad. Some letters contained as many as two hundred titles.

That was the start, and the flow of correspondence has continued more or less unabated. Now, after fifteen years, I can perhaps claim to have an accurate impression of the musical taste of my audience.

What is that taste? On the whole it is for music that is sentimental, melodic, nostalgic and evocative, a tendency which I thought at first may have been due to the time of day of the programme, a reflection of the mood of the hour. But it was soon evident that the transmission time was not particularly responsible, and 'Your Hundred Best Tunes' could be accepted as a fair representation of the 'people's choice'. As one listener put it, this was 'music that speaks to us in straightforward terms'. Was she perhaps echoing Leopold Stokowski's dictum: 'Music comes from the heart and returns to the heart'?

When a radio programme has been running for a considerable time, as this one has, and prompted thousands of letters, the relationship becomes a very personal one, and you are bound to develop a rapport with your listeners. When the time comes to say 'Good evening', I am mindful of a Mrs Vickers, the Reverend Brown, the boys' club that switches off the television at nine o'clock to listen to the music; the tycoon whose name frequently appears in the press and who writes regularly to ask what records to buy; the old, blind lady in Huddersfield, the convent in Essex, a number of well-known politicians, a family in Norway and a man who supports Everton and sends a bombardment of musical notes of his own. Neither must I forget the lady who wrote, 'And to think we might never have known about your programme if our television hadn't broken down'. The correspondence has shown that this programme of 'Pops for Squares', as the *Radio Times* once called it, has wide appeal to listeners of all ages and in all walks of life. Especially have I been pleased to receive requests for the list of 'top tunes' from a number of local education authorities, whose intention it was to use it as a starting point for a new musical appreciation curriculum.

This communication with my unseen audience has been my most gratifying experience during many years in radio. Once when I returned to the air after a short break following the first series which had lasted several years, I felt as if I were coming home. I knew that my friends were waiting out there to greet me and I just had to say so.

It is to them that I address myself in the following pages in the hope that they will find something interesting in these sketches about the music that they themselves have shown to be amongst the most popular. I begin, as the programme begins, with the signature tune.

Signature Tune

The Londonderry Air

From County Derry, this Irish tune is one of the most familiar of all folk melodies. Sir Hubert Parry, no mean composer himself, thought it the most beautiful tune in the world, and John McCormack, who was of the same opinion about it, used to tell this story: 'Once when I was in Londonderry I asked an old fiddler there if he knew its origin and he said, "Now John, you've come to the right man for 'twas myself that found it and this is how it came about. I'd been playing at a wedding and after I had drunk the health of the bride and groom a couple of times I set off home. On the way I got tired and sat down in the moonlight under a cock o' hay and fell asleep. I was awakened by the loveliest melody, and when I opened my eyes, there before me was a leprechaun orchestra, and they playing away. I took a bit of music paper and set down what they were playing and fell asleep again. And I woke in the morning with the sun beaming down in my eyes and I took my fiddle and I played the tune that I jotted down from the fairy orchestra, and would you believe it, John, it was the Londonderry Air itself."'

A delightful tale; but the origin of the tune is, of course, unknown. It was apparently taken down for the first time in Limavady in County Derry in 1851. The best arrangement of it for orchestra is Percy Grainger's.

'Abide with Me'

One of the best-loved hymns in the English language, the verses of 'Abide with Me' were written by Henry Francis Lyte (1793–1847), the vicar of Brixham in Devon, when he was close to death. He preached what was to be his last sermon on 5 September 1847, and on his return home the words came to him, and the lines were published in a leaflet in Brixham later that month.

The tune, called 'Eventide', was composed by William Henry Monk (1823–99) for the first edition of *Hymns Ancient and Modern* in 1861, of which he was the editor.

Both words and tune have given comfort for almost as long as they have been written; and the following story, which appeared in a Scottish newspaper, the *Sunday Post*, some years ago gives just one example.

'In a quiet corner of Lochee, Dundee, last Sunday an old woman lay dying. Her daughter Nettie sat with her, holding her hand and stroking her hair; both knew the end was near. It had been months since the old mother had been able to leave her home, and again and again she had asked Nettie to read her the words of her favourite hymn, 'Abide with Me', and Nettie had done so because they brought her mother so much comfort.

'Then, just as the hands of the clock crept to 10 p.m., a remarkable thing happened. Through the open window, clear as a bell, came the sound of a magnificent tenor voice singing the very hymn which had given the old lady such strength.

> *Hold thou Thy cross before my closing eyes,*
> *Shine through the gloom and point me to the skies;*
> *Heaven's morning breaks, and earth's vain shadows flee,*
> *In life and death, O Lord, abide with me.*

'As the last word rang out, Nettie's mother closed her eyes, smiling peacefully, and a little before midnight she died.'

What was the explanation? Nettie learned next day that a neighbour had come in and switched on her radio, hoping to hear the news. Instead she found herself listening to 'Your Hundred Best Tunes' and Sunday's last item had been 'Abide with Me'.

ADOLPHE ADAM

(1803–1856)

Born in Paris, Adolphe Adam was perhaps the most admired comic opera and ballet composer of his time, and his melodies were heard throughout Europe. He first achieved international notice with *Le Postillon de Longjumeau*, which was regarded as the most charming light opera of the period, and notable mainly for the principal tenor aria, which afforded the singer an excellent opportunity to exercise his bravura on one of the highest notes in the vocal range: top D.

Fifty-three operas bear Adam's name, and yet we hear hardly anything today beyond an overture or two. He is chiefly remembered for his ballet *Giselle*.

First presented at the Paris Opera in 1841 this was an instantaneous success. Though by no means the oldest ballet performed today, it is the earliest of all the 'classics' and a permanent fixture in international ballet repertoire. Its best-known melodies are the Waltz in Act I, and the Grand *pas de deux* and Variations towards the end of the second Act when the final dramatic moments are being played out. A critic at one of its earliest performances was quite carried away: 'The blue rays of moonlight glide mysteriously over the silvery notes of its music' attested to his feelings.

One of Adam's songs which is particularly popular at Christmas is 'O Holy Night', an English translation of the 'Cantique de Noël', which was first sung at midnight mass on Christmas Eve in 1847. But French ecclesiastical authorities banned it from their services for almost a hundred years as being 'totally without the spirit of religion'. It has now come back into its own.

TOMMASO ALBINONI

(1671–1750)

A Venetian composer and violinist who was pleased to describe himself as a 'dilettante', a modest description for one whose output included at least forty-nine operas which were reputedly very successful in their time. As a composer of instrumental music Albinoni was greatly admired by his contemporary, Johann Sebastian Bach, who made arrangements of two of his fugues.

Albinoni is mentioned here because of one piece that suddenly appeared on the musical scene in the early nineteen-sixties, Adagio for Organ and Strings in G Minor. The person responsible for its introduction was Remo Giazotto, an Italian musicologist. He brought to light the fragment of a sonata attributed to Albinoni said to have been found in the ruins of an old library in Dresden which was destroyed by bombing in World War II. Giazotto reconstructed this fragment to make the Adagio a piece of sustained melody that immediately appealed to public fancy. It has become one of the numbers most requested on my programme. Though denounced in some quarters as 'spurious', there is no doubt that this piece has brought Albinoni's name to a much wider audience than ever before.

'All in the April Evening'

Often requested by listeners, this is undoubtedly the most popular song of those made famous by the Glasgow Orpheus Choir, conducted by Sir Hugh Roberton (1874–1952) for nearly half a

14

century. Sir Hugh was also the composer of the setting of this song, based on a poem called 'Sheeps and Lambs' by the Irish poetess Katherine Tynan.

GREGORIO ALLEGRI
(1582–1652)

Here is a case where I can modestly claim that 'Your Hundred Best Tunes' has significantly helped to popularize a work known previously only to devoted followers of choral music. Allegri's *Miserere* became popular to the extent that in the nationwide poll of listeners' favourite music in 1970, it occupied thirteenth place in the votes cast.

Born in Rome, Allegri began his association with the Church as a boy chorister. He later entered the Papal Choir as a tenor, having already earned a small reputation as the composer of some motets. The *Miserere*, a setting of the fifty-first Psalm for nine solo voices and two choirs, brought fame to Allegri. One of the most beautiful compositions in all church music, it is a customary part of Holy Week celebrations at St Peter's, Rome. It became the exclusive property of the Papal Choir, and was at one time so jealously guarded and cherished that even to copy it was a crime worth the punishment of excommunication.

There is a well-known story of the young Mozart at fourteen. While visiting Rome during Holy Week he heard the *Miserere* in the Sistine Chapel, and immediately after the service wrote out the whole complicated work from memory, an interesting sidelight on music once described as 'the sound of Heaven'.

JOHANN SEBASTIAN BACH

(1685–1750)

It could be said that Bach in his lifetime altered the whole concept of music and had a strong influence on musical thought thereafter. Robert Schumann did not think he was exaggerating when he said that 'music owes as much to Bach as Christianity to Christ'.

Yet the music of Johann Sebastian faded into oblivion within a few years after his death, and the name of Bach was almost always taken to mean his sons Johann Christian and Carl Philipp Emanuel, both of whom were successful composers in their own right. By comparison, few people recalled their father, and then probably as an organist rather than a composer. For many years his work lay unremembered and hardly ever performed.

The list of Bach's works is vast. In 1850, the centenary of the year of his death, a society was formed to perpetuate his name and his music. Having undertaken to collate everything he had written, ten scholars took almost fifty years to complete the task—which only included everything that could be found. There had been a time when manuscripts of his were being sold for the equivalent of a few pence.

Bach was born in Eisenach in Germany. His first instrument was the violin which he learnt from his father, a well-known town musician. When Johann Sebastian was ten years old both his parents died and he went to live with his elder brother, Johann Christoph, who introduced him to keyboard instruments of which he readily became an eager and talented pupil. Avid to advance his knowledge, but unable to get at volumes of music by contemporary composers to which his brother had forbidden access, Johann Sebastian secretly and by the light of the moon spent night after night laboriously copying the books of organ music he so much wanted to study.

Bach's first post was as violinist in a court orchestra, but within a year, at the age of eighteen, he had become organist at a church in Arnstadt. This marked the beginning of a career that led in 1708 to his appointment as organist at the Ducal Chapel in Weimar, the first of the three periods that were important landmarks in his life.

Bach was married twice and had twenty children. His first wife died in 1720 and a year later he married Anna Magdalena, the daughter of a court trumpeter. She was also a cultured musician and singer, and contributed greatly to Bach's happy domestic life.

His finest period began in 1723 when he was appointed cantor at St Thomas's Church in Leipzig. This enabled him to continue as church organist, to train the choir and to compose music for the services. It was here in Leipzig that he wrote his greatest religious works.

Towards the end of his life his eyesight caused him grave concern. It had always been weak, and he submitted to an unsuccessful operation which resulted in total blindness. By some miracle his sight was suddenly, partially restored, but within a very short time his world became dark again. On 18 July 1750 he suffered a stroke, and ten days later the great Johann Sebastian Bach was dead.

Considering Bach's prodigious treasury of musical output it is an invidious task to have to choose a mere handful of works to write about here. For the purpose of this book, however, I must only be concerned with the music which, in the widest sense, is the most popular.

'Jesu, Joy of Man's Desiring' comes from the Church Cantata no. 147, 'Herz und Mund und Tat und Leben' ('Heart and mouth and deed and life'), composed in Weimar in 1716 for the service of Visitation. The chorale which closes each of the two parts of the Cantata is known as 'Jesu, meiner Seelen Wonne'. Of the many English translations, the following by Robert Bridges is perhaps the most popular.

> *Jesu, Joy of man's desiring,*
> *Holy wisdom, love most bright.*
> *Drawn by Thee, our souls aspiring,*
> *Soar to uncreated light.*
> *Word of God, our flesh that fashioned,*
> *With the fire of life impassioned,*
> *Striving still to Truth unknown,*
> *Soaring, dying round Thy Throne.*

Through the way where Hope is guiding,
Hark, what peaceful music rings.
Where the flock, in Thee confiding,
Drink of joy from deathless springs.
Theirs is beauty's fairest pleasure;
Theirs is wisdom's holiest treasure;
Thou dost ever lead Thine own,
In the love of joys unknown.

(Copyright 1931 OUP)

It might be said that the tune was made famous by the version transcribed for piano by Dame Myra Hess, which she frequently played at her National Gallery lunch-time concerts during the Second World War. It has been popular ever since and is one of the most widely known of all Bach's pieces.

'Sheep May Safely Graze' was also written in 1716 as an aria for soprano and two flutes, and is from Bach's first known Secular Cantata, the *Hunting* or *Birthday* Cantata, no. 208. It was composed for the birthday celebrations of Duke Christian of Saxe-Weissenfels, and performed as banquet music at the duke's hunting lodge after a day's hunt.

The lovely aria 'Schafe Können Sicher Weiden' is the one celebrated part of the work whose music transports us at once to a pastoral scene of sheer delight, and one of many translations is:

Sheep may safely graze all fearless,
Where a shepherd guards them well.
So the nation ruled in wisdom
Knows and shares the many blessings
Which both peace and plenty bring.

There are a number of orchestral versions of this melody, the best of which is that by Sir William Walton in his ballet 'The Wise Virgins' for the Sadler's Wells Company.

'Wachet Auf' ('Sleepers Wake') Cantata no. 140. Of the three hundred or so cantatas composed by Bach, this is perhaps the best known, particularly because of the fourth section, the tenor chorale 'Zion hört die Wächter Singen' ('Zion hears her watchmen's voices') through which flows one of the most beautiful of string melodies. Equally well known is the title chorus 'Wachet Auf'.

The Cantata was composed in about 1731 for the twenty-seventh Sunday after Trinity or thereabouts, the reading for the day being the parable of the wise and foolish virgins. The work itself is based on a hymn by Philipp Nicolai published in 1599. 'Wachet Auf' in Bach's own arrangement is also one of the most favoured of his chorale preludes and there exist several transcriptions for orchestra, Leopold Stokowski's being best known.

'Bist du Bei mir' ('If thou art near') is a song from the two notebooks of Anna Magdalena, the treasured and decorated volumes that contained little keyboard pieces and songs put together by Bach for his wife's personal pleasure and, incidentally, for the musical education of their children. It is one of the most beautiful love songs I know, a simple and tender expression of devotion that one can imagine her singing to him alone.

> *If thou art near me*
> *How happy would be my end*
> *To have thy beautiful hands*
> *Close my eyes.*

Sadly, it is now thought that the song was not written by Bach, but by an obscure composer from Saxony called Gottfried Heinrich Stölzel. But even that in no way diminishes the beauty of this lovely song.

Toccata and Fugue in D Minor is a mighty showpiece dating from Bach's earlier days in Weimar. Undoubtedly the most popular of all his organ compositions, it has been the subject of various theories. André Pirro, a Bach historian, suggested that the Toccata contained all the elements of a 'classic storm—dazzling lightning, claps of thunder rumbling formidably . . . the wind, then the hail'. The fugue begins serenely, the calm before another storm, grows in intensity and finally matches the Toccata in its powerful and majestic climax.

There have been numerous orchestral arrangements of the work, notably by Eugene Ormandy and Leopold Stokowski. Sir Henry Wood also produced an orchestral version and presented it at a Promenade Concert at the Queen's Hall in 1929. The programme attributed the transcription to a Russian musician called Paul Klenovsky—Sir Henry's own pseudonym!

This 'little joke', as Wood referred to it, was mentioned in his autobiography. 'Glazunov had visited me and told me of the death of a promising young pupil of his by the name of Klenovsky, a name which took my fancy . . . Klenovsky's success was unquestioned. Every season it is asked for and still finds a place in Promenade programmes.' The truth was only revealed when a publisher approached Sir Henry for Klenovsky's address. He wanted to obtain permission to publish the work.

The Air, from Suite no. 3 for Orchestra in D Major, was composed for Duke Leopold's chamber ensemble at Cöthen which Bach usually directed from the harpsichord. The preference of the general public for this particular one of the four Suites for orchestra rests solely on its second movement, the famous Air, which is a marvel of melodic beauty that must be in everyone's list of best tunes. It is a movement of calm solemnity for solo strings.

The Air reached a much wider audience when August Wilhelmji, a German violinist, arranged it for violin and piano. He transposed the melody to a lower register and called it Air on the G string.

Concerto for Two Violins in D Minor: much of Bach's violin music has unfortunately been lost, although three concertos still survive. These are the ones he left to his son, Carl Philipp Emanuel, the most popular of which is the Double Concerto for Two Violins and String Orchestra. The heart of the concerto is doubtless the tranquil middle movement, a beautiful, flowing duet which is quite exceptional. Its virtue was perhaps best stated by the critic who said that although 'the two violins are used as independent voices, they speak with a most moving eloquence'. They weave a stream of melody that has been described as 'a heavenly meditation'. It is on account of this movement in particular that this concerto stands so high in the ranks of music for the violin.

The *Passion according to St John*. Bach is believed to have written five Passions, but only two complete ones remain. St John is the earlier one which he wrote while still at Cöthen during the winter of 1722–3. Though his appointment as cantor at St Thomas's Church, Leipzig, had been confirmed, he might well have used this as a sort of test piece with which to introduce himself to the good burghers of the city, and he had little more than ten weeks in which to complete the work.

The text that Bach used was not based entirely on the Evangelist's stories. He joined the words of the Gospel with some fragments of a German poem, 'Jesus Martyred and dying for the Sins of the World', a text that Handel had used earlier. He also included appropriate verses from old hymns, even retaining the original melodies. Bach blended these sources which, combined with his genius, gave us dramatic music at its finest.

Dr Albert Schweitzer's is the last word. He wrote that 'the brooding tenderness and deep compassion with which Bach describes and meditates upon the incomparable drama are reflected in page after page of poignant beauty'.

The *Passion according to St Matthew*. In the eighteenth century it was the practice at Leipzig to perform a different Passion setting each year on Good Friday. Bach by this time had been cantor at St Thomas's for six years; Good Friday had come round again and Johann Sebastian had prepared for them his Passion according to St Matthew.

On the day, however, many of the citizens of Leipzig preferred to attend another church to hear a Passion by a very indifferent composer. Those who chose to savour Bach's work sat there in bewilderment. It was thought to be too 'theatrical', and they didn't hesitate to voice their complaints. One noble lady in the congregation is reported to have said: 'God save us, my children, it's just as if one were at an opera comedy.'

Although this rendering of the *Passion* was greatly misunderstood at the time, it received several more performances under Bach's direction in later years. But like so much of his other music, it remained forgotten after his death until the enthusiasm of Mendelssohn, a devoted admirer of Bach from his youth, led to a revival of this masterpiece. With the help of some friends, including a well-known actor of the day, Mendelssohn arranged a performance in Berlin on Good Friday 1829, one hundred years after its first unhappy presentation at St Thomas's. Mendelssohn himself conducted the resurrected *St Matthew Passion*. It was so well received by the public that his joy in its success prompted him to announce proudly that 'it was an actor and a Jew who restored this great Christian work to the people'.

LUDWIG VAN BEETHOVEN

(1770–1827)

In his very early years Beethoven showed a strong dislike of music. Though an unwilling pupil under his father's harsh tutorship, by the time he was seven he was a very good pianist and already performing in public.

When he was seventeen, Beethoven visited Vienna where Mozart was asked to hear him play. His improvisation on a theme that the great composer gave him elicited a spontaneous verdict from Mozart: 'Mind my word, this young man will make a name for himself.'

In 1795 Beethoven left his native Bonn to settle in Vienna, which was then the great musical centre of Europe and where he was to spend the rest of his life; a life that for much of the time was beset by worries about money and ill health. Despite his success as a composer and as the greatest of virtuoso pianists, his blissful moments were few. And when in 1801 he became partially deaf, he said in a letter to a friend: 'I cannot fail to be the most unhappy of God's creatures.'

But though he was always poor he never forgot to be generous. For a concert given in aid of wounded soldiers, a performance in which Spohr, Meyerbeer and Hummel also took part, he supplied music and conducted. When an offer of payment was made, his retort was: 'Say Beethoven never accepts anything where humanity is concerned.' Most of what money he earned went to doctors in the vain hope of their finding a cure for his increasing deafness. But in 1802 his hearing had completely left him. From then on, the music that his ears denied him he heard in his mind.

When it is said of Beethoven that he was morose, churlish and ill-tempered, it indicates a failure to recognize the courage that shines through his music, and that, in the midst of his suffering, he never lost the devotion to all that was highest in his art.

In England his music commanded widespread interest. Broadwood sent him one of their latest pianos as a token of their esteem, and among his greatest admirers were members of the Philharmonic Society who invited him to London a number of times, without success. When they heard, early in 1827, that Beethoven was seriously ill, they sent him a hundred pounds, 'to be applied to his comforts and necessities during his illness'. Even in his weakened state he replied to say that he was touched by their generosity, and promised to send them his tenth symphony which, as we know, was never to be written. Neither was he able to use their money, for he died a few days later.

In an old music book, I came across this moving paragraph recording the closing hours of Beethoven's life: 'In the afternoon of March 26th, 1827, Beethoven was seized with his last mortal faintness. Thick clouds were hanging about the sky. Outside, the snow lay upon the ground and towards evening the wind rose; at nightfall a terrific thunderstorm burst over the city of Vienna and, whilst the storm was still raging, the spirit of the sublime master departed.'

In noting some of Beethoven's music that I have included in my programme, it would perhaps be appropriate to begin with the Symphony no. 3 in E Flat (*Eroica*) which contains the great funeral march. Some contend that this symphony was inspired by Beethoven's strong idealism and faith in humanity. He saw Napoleon Bonaparte as a liberator, for instance, and it was to him that he dedicated this work.

But Beethoven's illusions were shattered when news reached him that Napoleon had declared himself Emperor. He felt betrayed, and in a fit of rage declared that 'Now he too will trample on the rights of men and indulge only his ambitions'. Disappointed, he called him a tyrant and angrily tore the title-page and its dedication from the manuscript. When later it was published the symphony bore as a replacement dedication: 'An heroic symphony to celebrate the memory of a great man.'

First performed in public in 1805, the symphony was not altogether favourably received, either by the critics or the audience. One listener in the gallery shouted down: 'I'd give another *kreuzer* [a silver coin] if only they'd stop.'

But whatever the opinions of the time and the many interpretations put upon the work, it remained Beethoven's own favourite symphony.

Symphony no. 5 in C Minor has an opening which is probably as familiar to most audiences as their own national anthem. For some this is doubtless because, during the Second World War, the opening rhythm (which corresponds to the 'V' sign (· · · —) in Morse code) was used on the radio and elsewhere as a victory signal. As a result of this the symphony was also nicknamed 'Victory'.

The symphony had its first performance in 1808, although Beethoven began his sketches for it at least three years earlier. He interpreted the repetition of the four notes at the beginning of the first movement as 'Fate knocking at the door'. Others have suggested that the symphony expresses in musical terms Man's struggle with his destiny. However that may be, it is once again Beethoven's underlying concern for the freedom of man which emerges as a strong theme.

In the all-Beethoven programme at the Theater-an-der-Wien, still a popular theatre in Vienna, it was received with the greatest enthusiasm, and a fellow composer who was present at the time said: 'It was marvellous. It so bewildered me that when I went to put on my hat I couldn't find my head!'

Symphony no. 6 in F Major (*Pastoral*). Beethoven was passionately fond of the countryside, and would leave Vienna as often as he could in the summer to seek peace and sunlight in the little country town of Heiligenstadt. We know what this meant to him from his own comments, 'O God, in such a forest, on the heights, is found peace for Thy service', and 'It is as though every tree speaks to me'.

Composed at Heiligenstadt in 1808—the year of the first performance of the fifth symphony—the *Pastoral* Symphony expresses Beethoven's sensitive feelings for the wonders of nature. He subtitled the work 'Reflections of life in the country', and gave descriptive headings to each of the five movements. The first recalls the 'Awakening of joyful feelings on arriving in the country', and the next is a 'Scene by the brook', followed by a 'Merry gathering of country folk'. The fourth movement he entitled 'Thunderstorm', and the final and best-loved 'Happy and thankful feelings after the storm'. He called this 'The Shepherd's Song', and it is indeed a hymn of joy.

Berlioz was affected by this symphony more profoundly than by any of the others, likening it to a landscape that might have been painted by Michelangelo.

Symphony no. 7 in A Major was written four years after the *Pastoral*, and Beethoven regarded it as one of his best works. At its performance in the large hall of the University of Vienna it met with remarkable success. But according to Spohr, 'the performance gave extraordinary pleasure in spite of often ridiculous conducting by Beethoven': his deafness prevented him hearing all but the loud tones and at one time he was ten to twelve bars behind the orchestra. The *allegretto* was the audience's favourite movement and they clamoured for, and received, an encore. It has remained one of the most popular movements in all Beethoven's symphonies.

Many have attempted to explain what Beethoven may have had in mind when he wrote this symphony and perhaps because Wagner and others saw it as the glorification of the Dance, it is sometimes referred to as the *Dance* Symphony, an appellation that can only fit the *allegretto* as a 'dance of death'. Some have perceived in its haunting sadness and its hushed, deliberate measures a procession through the catacombs, but an acute rhythmic quality pervades the whole work that could also, at times, suggest wild and primitive dance forms.

Symphony no. 9 in D Minor. For twenty-five years Beethoven was obsessed with the desire to compose a setting for Schiller's 'Ode to Joy', a poem he had known and revered from his youth and a hymn that inspired his own ideas of the brotherhood of Man, the gist of which might be expressed in these few lines:

> *Be embraced, O ye millions;*
> *Brothers, above the starry heavens*
> *A loving father surely dwells.*

> *All men shall be brothers;*
> *When Thy gentle wing is spread*
> *Thy magic doth unite once more . . .*

(Translation by Peggie Cochrane)

As his sketch-books show, it was not until 1817 that Beethoven began to establish the form that the symphony would take. Instrumental music would not be enough; he would also need the human voice. The greatest critics have agreed that 'a nobler or more enduring tune than the great theme of the finale does not exist'.

The symphony was originally intended for the Philharmonic Society of London (for which a formal agreement had been drawn up in 1822), but it was Vienna that heard it first, on 7 May 1824. It was announced that 'Herr Michael Umlauf will conduct the entire performance, and Herr Ludwig van Beethoven will take part in conducting'. Those present at the concert in fact saw Beethoven, resplendent in formal evening dress, black silk knee breeches and silk stockings, standing in front of the orchestra and beating time. Behind him stood Umlauf who was actually conducting and the one whom the orchestra actually followed.

When the last notes of the symphony died away to tumultuous applause, Beethoven was still beating time. With tears in her eyes, one of the soloists affectionately took his arm and turned him to face the audience to receive the ovation he could not hear. For a moment he stood and looked straight out into the auditorium, bowed slowly and left the platform.

Piano Concerto no. 5 in E Flat Major (*Emperor*). This time the nickname *Emperor* had nothing to do with Napoleon. On the contrary, when Beethoven was working on the concerto the French army was battering the gates of Vienna. Deep in despair, Beethoven retreated from the noise of guns by hiding himself in a cellar and burying his head in a pillow.

The 'Emperor' title is credited to the English composer and piano maker J. B. Cramer who, it is said, happened to refer to this concerto as 'an Emperor among concertos', and it is doubtful whether the term had any more significance than that.

Completed in 1809, it was two years before any interest was shown in the work. This happened first in Leipzig where, according to a contemporary review, 'the crowded audience was put into a state of enthusiasm. . . . This is without doubt one of the most original, imaginative and effective of all existing concertos.' When it was played in Vienna, however, a year later, it was included in a hotchpotch of a concert, a benefit performance put on by a Charitable Society of Noble Ladies. Karl Czerny conducted, the same Czerny whose name so many of us knew as music students for his piano studies. Squeezed between a welter of 'acts' and tableaux, this masterly work had no chance to put the audience into a state of enthusiasm. It was not an affair to attract the music lovers that Beethoven cared for. A notice of the concert actually said that 'he can be understood and appreciated only by connoisseurs'.

Piano Sonata in C Minor (*Pathétique*), to whose powerful opening chords musicologists point as Beethoven's expression of an impending grief. Alarming signs of his deafness were to appear a year or two later. Then comes the first theme which may be seen as a defiant challenge and explained by a remark made by Beethoven in a letter to a friend: 'I shall seize Fate by the throat. It shall certainly not overcome me!'

27

By contrast, the *adagio* of the second movement might be regarded as a nocturnal poem. The Beethoven authority Marion Scott sums it up as 'a tragedy as the young might feel it, with the glamour, even the exaltation of a Romeo and Juliet. Few love scenes could be more softly glowing than this slow movement with its almost unbelievable melodic loveliness and velvety tone'. Of the three movements, this is perhaps the most popular.

Piano Sonata in C Sharp Minor (*Moonlight*), of which only the dreamy poetry of the first movement could possibly suggest 'moonlight'. Beethoven had nothing to do with the designation, but legend has it that a critic of the time had said that the shimmering serenity of the music suggested Lake Lucerne in the moonlight. Karl Czerny, of whom we have already spoken, called the first movement a nocturnal scene with a ghostly voice sounding in the distance.

Beethoven dedicated the sonata to a former pupil of his, a countess with whom he was deeply in love, and it was hinted that the composition was woven round his passion for her.

But while none of the numerous explanations can be taken seriously, it may be that the 'moonlight' title has contributed to the sonata's general popularity.

Albumblatt—Für Elise, a graceful little piano piece and the most famous of Beethoven's Bagatelles. The manuscript bears the inscription, 'For Elise on 27 April in remembrance of Ludwig van Beethoven'. It was later decided that it was really intended for a young lady named Therese whom the composer had hoped to marry, and that the mythical Elise owes her immortality to an error in deciphering Beethoven's illegible handwriting. As it sounds, it might well have been a birthday present, and none more delightful.

Egmont Overture. Apart from the symphonies, Beethoven's overtures are probably his most important orchestral works, and the overture to *Egmont* is one of several that are with us today as concert favourites.

Beethoven's imagination had been fired by the theme of Goethe's poetic drama, *Egmont*, the theme of a nation's struggle for liberation—here once again he was taking up the cause of freedom. In 1810 he supplied nine pieces as incidental music for a new production at the Burgtheater in Vienna. The overture, in effect a symphonic poem, superbly summarizes the tragedy of the Dutch people in their fight against Spanish oppression. As leader of the rebellion, Egmont was executed as the result of a vile conspiracy, but in death as in life he remained the hero of the struggle. Divided into three sections, the overture depicts in turn oppression, conflict and, in a most powerful climax, ultimate victory.

The Violin Concerto in D Major is Beethoven's only violin concerto, but one of the most beautiful and important ever composed. It was written for Franz Clement, a remarkable violinist who, at its first performance, undauntedly played the concerto at sight. Beethoven had retained the manuscript almost up to the time of performance in order to make last-minute revisions. Nevertheless Clement's performance ensured a most enthusiastic reception for the concerto, although one dissenting voice, annoyed at Beethoven's use of the kettledrum, sneeringly referred to the work as 'the *Kettledrum* Concerto'.

Clement, great violinist though he was, was not above comic and pretentious displays on the platform. At this same concert he also played a sonata (sometimes called a fantasia) of his own on one string with the violin upside-down!

The three movements of the D Major concerto are a veritable outpouring of melodic ideas, particularly the lyrical *larghetto* of the second movement. And the cheerful *rondo*, said to be based on a Russian folk tune, makes for a brilliant endpiece.

Missa Solemnis in D Major is a masterpiece which occupied Beethoven's thoughts for over four years. He began to plan it in 1818 for performance at the enthronement of his former pupil,

Rudolf, Archduke of Austria, as Archbishop of Olmütz in March 1820. But the Mass proved a far more arduous task than he had anticipated, and reached such massive proportions that it was not completed for a further two years after the ceremony for which it had originally been intended. Music by Haydn and Hummel was used in its place.

Beethoven's Mass is one of his most ambitious works and contains some of his most profoundly affecting music. He explained that his chief object in the composition of this Grand Mass was to awaken in and deeply impress religious feelings upon both singers and hearers. As if to emphasize the humanity of the work, he wrote over the *Kyrie* in the original manuscript: 'From the heart—may it reach the heart.'

VINCENZO BELLINI

(1801–1835)

Bellini came of a musical family. His father and grandfather had been organists at the cathedral in Catania in Sicily where he was born. He received his early musical education from his father but, at the age of eighteen, supported financially by a Sicilian nobleman who had recognized his talent, Vincenzo attended the Conservatory at Naples and later studied briefly with Haydn, Mozart and Pergolesi.

While still at the Conservatory he composed an opera that attracted the attention of the impresario of the San Carlo Company of Naples, who commissioned him to write an opera for that house. That was in 1826. Four years were to elapse before success arrived in the form of an opera based on the story of Romeo and Juliet. This was produced at La Fenice in Venice, and although it was acclaimed a masterpiece, even then Bellini was not widely recognized until he had composed *La Sonnambula*, followed one year later by *Norma*.

Bellini's music stands with the best in Italian opera. He was unrivalled in his gift of lyricism, and his graceful melodies have

never failed to please the music public. He died in Paris on 25
September 1835.

La Sonnambula ('The Sleepwalker') was first presented in 1831.
Bellini's happiest work, no opera was more popular in the last
century—it was Queen Victoria's favourite too. In London,
Jenny Lind, who was known as the 'Swedish nightingale', sang
the role of Amina, the girl who walks in her sleep, on twenty-two
occasions. Among the best-known numbers from the opera are
the soprano cavatina 'Come per me sereno', 'Prendi l'anel ti
dono', and 'Ah! non credea mirarti'. This last was said to have
been Chopin's favourite melody, and one of the many legends has
it that in his dying moments he asked for it to be played to him.

Norma, the tragic opera which Bellini regarded as his finest
achievement, was a failure at its first performance at La Scala,
Milan, in 1831. In Bellini's own words it was 'a fiasco, a serious
fiasco'. In fact it took several years for *Norma* to receive the
recognition it so justly deserved. The most famous tune from this
opera—and indeed one of the most celebrated of all operatic arias
—is 'Casta Diva', a prayer to the 'Chaste Goddess'. 'Mira O
Norma', a duet for soprano and contralto, is also very beautiful
indeed.

I Puritani was Bellini's last opera and had its première in Paris in
January 1835, at the Théâtre des Italiens where Rossini was the
director. It had come about as the result of an invitation from
Rossini to come to Paris and write an opera expressly for his
theatre. While not the best of Bellini's work, and marred also by
a poor libretto, the opera nevertheless contains many pages of
great lyrical beauty, notably the tenor aria 'Ah te O Cara' and the
exquisite 'Qui la voce'.

At the end of 1835, *I Puritani* was again performed in Paris,
opening on the eve of Bellini's funeral. Journals of the time wrote
that sobbing was heard throughout the entire performance, the

singers, orchestra and audience being quite overcome with grief. At the end of the evening the cast and orchestra, under the direction of Rossini and Cherubini, joined in a Requiem Mass for the dead composer at the Church of Les Invalides.

HECTOR BERLIOZ
(1803–1869)

Berlioz was one of the most original and complex figures in musical history. He was an innovator who defied the conventions of his craft and, in his own words, 'took up music where Beethoven left it'. Though he is recognized today as the greatest composer ever produced by France, his unconventional approach to music was resented and his critics were blunt. He was called 'a genius without talent'. Chopin, for instance, thought that Berlioz's music was such as to 'justify any man breaking relations with him'. Schumann was uncertain whether to label him genius or musical charlatan, and in later years Ravel referred to him as 'the worst musician of all the musical geniuses', and he added: 'He couldn't harmonize a simple waltz tune properly.'

Despite such acrimonious remarks you will notice that the word 'genius' keeps recurring, and this Berlioz undoubtedly was.

The son of a doctor, Berlioz was expected to follow in his father's footsteps, but he was so deeply interested in music that it was unwillingly and only out of a sense of filial duty that he attended medical school. His first sight of the dissecting room so horrified him that he fled from the place vowing never to return. But he resumed his medical studies at his father's insistence, for a short spell, until his musical leaning proved too strong for him.

He eventually overcame parental opposition to enter the Paris Conservatoire, by which time he had already produced a variety of compositions.

At the Conservatoire his striking talent was soon obvious, prompting one of his teachers to say to him, 'You will not be a doctor but a great composer because you have genius. I say it because it is true', a prediction that was partly fulfilled when Berlioz won the Prix de Rome, a famous prize awarded annually to outstanding young musicians. Before this, however, he had composed one of his finest works, the *Symphonie Fantastique*, despite which he was little thought of and had not yet succeeded in reaching a wider public, and his rewards were few. Not until 1834 with the production of his symphony *Harold in Italy*, and later his Great Mass, and the dramatic symphony *Romeo and Juliet*, did his fame spread throughout Europe.

For all the success that his music achieved, his life seemed to consist of nothing but disappointment and frustration. His two marriages both failed, adding to his bitterness, and Berlioz died a broken and lonely man on 9 March 1869.

Gounod and Ambroise Thomas were pall bearers at his funeral, and the procession was led by the Band of the National Guard which played the funeral march from his *Symphonie Funèbre et Triomphale*.

Symphonie Fantastique. The first performance took place at the Paris Conservatoire in 1830 to a very mixed reception indeed. Some hailed it as the 'new music', while others despised it.

The work arose out of Berlioz's overwhelming passion for Henrietta Smithson, an Irish actress who appeared in Paris for a season of Shakespeare plays. He had seen her as Ophelia and Juliet, and fallen madly in love with her. He wrote her letters which she ignored, thus denying him an opportunity to demonstrate his ardent feelings for her. A rumour that she was engaged to be married so intensely outraged him and made him so jealous that he felt impelled to express his unrequited love in this symphony.

Divided into five movements, the work is subtitled 'An episode in the life of an artist'. There is a melody running through it, a fixed motif which varies according to the mood of the piece, and each movement is described. The first he called 'Dreams and Passions', because it concerned the meeting of a young artist and the woman of his ideals, and the second is 'A Ball'. Through the music of a waltz he imagines he sees his Beloved again. Next is a country scene in which the vision of her brings him momentary repose and contentment, but in 'The March to the Scaffold' he believes he has killed his Beloved and is to be executed for his crime. The last movement depicts 'A Witches' Sabbath', an infernal orgy in which the Beloved melody is reduced to a grotesque and hideous travesty.

Despite all this expression of anguish, Berlioz did eventually marry Henrietta, a union that was miserable and short-lived.

❧❀❧

Le Carnaval Romain ('Roman Carnival') is a very popular work and frequently requested. Its history is brief.

After his opera *Benvenuto Cellini* had been performed without success, Berlioz, who had intended to compose a new prelude to the second act, reconsidered the matter because of the opera's failure and decided that there were parts of it worth saving which could be incorporated in an independent overture. He in fact rescued several tunes, notably a *saltarello* and a love melody, which both became prominent features of an overture that is regarded as the best of Berlioz's shorter works. Berlioz himself conducted its first performance in Paris in 1844, where it was so well received that it had to be repeated before the concert was allowed to continue.

❧❀❧

The *Damnation of Faust* is a concert opera dedicated to Franz Liszt, who had persuaded Berlioz to read Goethe's *Faust*. This so possessed him that it became, he said, a landmark in his life.

Over a number of years, Berlioz had composed settings for various scenes from the *Faust* legend, and in 1847 an opera both rich and diverse was ready for presentation. A chain of broadly conceived episodes rather than a minutely developed plot, it had at the time a mere two performances to half-empty houses and was pronounced a failure. Nowadays we are familiar with many orchestral excerpts taken from it, and three particular selections are often combined to make up a concert item: the *Dance of the Will of the Wisp*, the *Ballet of the Sylphs* and the *Hungarian (Racoczy) March*.

The famous *Hungarian (Racoczy) March* is thought to have been composed by a gipsy violinist, a court musician to the Transylvanian Prince Racoczy. It was eventually accepted as a piece of Hungarian folk music and, when Berlioz orchestrated it for a concert early in 1846, it created such a furore that he expediently set the first part of the *Damnation of Faust* in Hungary so that the march could be included.

L'Enfance du Christ ('Childhood of Christ') is an oratorio whose best-loved chorus is the 'Shepherds' Farewell to the Holy Family', and Berlioz has described in detail how he came to write this.

A friend had asked him to inscribe something in his album, whereupon Berlioz took a piece of paper and jotted down a series of notes, an *andantino* in four parts for the organ, a simple, tranquil melody. It was in fact a Lutheran chorale that happened to be in Berlioz's head at the time when a sudden desire took hold of him to add some words in the same vein. What was an organ piece became the chorus of the shepherds at Bethlehem bidding farewell to the Holy Family at their departure for Egypt. Known to us as 'Thou must leave thy lowly dwelling', this tender chorale with added material became the middle section of the *Childhood of Christ*.

GEORGES BIZET
(1838–1875)

According to one of his teachers at the Paris Conservatoire, Bizet possessed little trace of talent, and yet he won, at the early age of seventeen, the much-coveted Prix de Rome, a high honour in the world of music. At nineteen, with a one-act opera, he won first prize in a competition sponsored by Offenbach, but little was heard of him for another six years until he attracted some attention with *The Pearl Fishers*. The reception for this was hardly more than luke-warm and Bizet was no further on the road to success. Two operas that followed, and *The Fair Maid of Perth*, fared little better than his earlier efforts.

The year 1872 proved a turning point. He achieved a measure

of success with the incidental music he wrote for Daudet's play 'L'Arlésienne', and in the same year he received a commission from the Opéra-Comique to supply music for a new work based on a Spanish theme. The opera was *Carmen*, but Bizet did not live to see it hailed by the world as a masterpiece.

Carmen. There are varying accounts of the first performance of this opera; some say it was 'a flop', and others that it did moderately well. But whichever version is correct it still took three years to be established. Tchaikovsky forecast that within a decade it would be the most popular opera in the world.

Well-known music from *Carmen* includes 'Habañera' ('Love is like a wild bird'), which was not an original composition by Bizet but one which he took to be a Spanish folksong. It was, in fact, composed by Yradier. The famous 'Toréador Song' is sung after Escamillo has described the bull fight in detail and a crowd of admirers has followed him into the inn where they take up the refrain 'Toréador, en garde!' The 'Flower Song' ('La fleur que tu m'avais jetée') is Don José's reply to Carmen's accusation that he no longer loves her. He shows her the flower she had given him, as proof of his love.

Les Pêcheurs de Perles ('The Pearl Fishers') is set in ancient Ceylon and concerns the love of two men, Zurga, king of the pearl fishers, and his friend Nadir, for the same woman, the priestess Leila. Two songs that stand out particularly in a score of great charm are 'Au fond du temple saint' ('In the depths of the temple'), one of the most beautiful tenor-baritone duets in all opera, and 'Je crois entendre encore' ('I hear as in a dream'), a tenor aria of poignant beauty in which Nadir, a fisherman, tells of his re-awakened love.

L'Arlésienne Suites comprise the best of the music that Bizet wrote for the play by Daudet, which was later made into two suites. Among favoured tunes are the *Prelude*, a rousing march adapted from a Provençal folk tune, and the *Adagietto*, a lovely piece of music for muted strings that, in the play, accompanied a most touching conversation between an old shepherd and his sweetheart when both were young. Now, after fifty years, they meet again: 'Hold me close to your heart; I have longed these many years to give you this token of my affection.' The *Intermezzo* is a good, broad tune to which the words of the *Agnus Dei* were later added. It became a popular, sacred song to be performed by such tenors as Enrico Caruso and Beniamino Gigli.

'Blow the Wind Southerly'

This dates from the end of the seventeenth century and comes from Northumberland, although the song we know today is made up of fragments of various versions that were once heard on the docks of Tyneside as young women awaited the home-coming of their seafaring men. The tune, *Kinloch of Kinloch*, may well have strayed across the border from Scotland and is also popular as a country dance.

LUIGI BOCCHERINI
(1743–1805)

An Italian composer, born in Lucca where his career began as a 'cellist in the town theatre. Early success as a composer and performer took him on a tour of Europe. At the invitation of the French ambassador to Spain he settled in Madrid, where he spent the rest of his life. He achieved but a fleeting fame and died in poverty. Yet after his death, as is often the case, it was said of him that 'rarely had a composer the merit of originality to a greater degree than Boccherini'.

His musical output was prolific. He was responsible for twenty symphonies, 102 string quartets, four 'cello concertos and 125 string quintets. From one of these comes the famous Minuet, the only composition by which Boccherini is really remembered today. It comes from the String Quintet in E Major opus 13 no. 5, and is one of the most graceful pieces of its kind, widely popular with string orchestras.

ALEXANDER BORODIN

(1833–1887)

Borodin was a distinguished professor of chemistry, and his music career, though highly successful, can only be said to have been that of an amateur.

He showed musical talent early and was mainly self-taught. By the age of ten he could play several instruments, and had already composed some small pieces. His mother encouraged his musical interest, and summoned a member of the local regimental band to teach her son the flute. He proved an exceptional pupil, and within two years had a number of serious compositions to his credit, including a concerto for flute and piano. His tuition continued with a famous teacher, until he became a medical student.

In 1862, at the time of his appointment to an assistant professorship at the Academy of Sciences in St Petersburg, he met Balakirev, who was then at the centre of a movement to revive an interest in Russian national music. Inspired by Balakirev's fervent advocacy, Borodin became an active member of the 'Five' who were working to that end. The 'Five', or the 'Mighty Handful' as they were also known, included Rimsky-Korsakov, César Cui and Mussorgsky as well. From that time Borodin's life followed the parallel paths of science and music, with just as much time devoted to each. He once wrote: 'I can only compose when I am too unwell to give my lectures. So my friends, reversing the usual custom, never say to me, "I hope you are well" but rather, "I do hope you are ill".' The music by which Borodin is best remembered includes the opera *Prince Igor*.

Prince Igor. For a long time Borodin had nursed an ambition to write an essentially Russian opera. He chose as his subject a legend from Russian history of the twelfth century, and on and off for about seventeen years he worked at it. At his death, however, it remained unfinished, and Rimsky-Korsakov and his pupil Glazunov completed the work. The overture, which had never been written down, was orchestrated from memory by Glazunov who had often heard Borodin play it on the piano, and the complete opera was first presented in St Petersburg in 1890, three years after the composer's death.

The most celebrated section of the opera is the set of *Polovetsian Dances*, frequently heard in the concert hall and sometimes with chorus. The dances are part of the festivities provided by the Polovetsians, a Tartar race, in honour of their captive, Prince Igor. The music begins with the sensuous melody of the slave girls, and with the entrance of the warriors it mounts to fever pitch and a thrilling finale.

In the Steppes of Central Asia is an orchestral sketch. Written in 1880 and dedicated to Franz Liszt, it was originally intended to accompany a series of tableaux at the celebrations of the twenty-fifth anniversary of the reign of Czar Alexander II. In a preface to the score Borodin described the piece. A caravan escorted by Russian soldiers is crossing the vast desert of Central Asia. The silence is broken by singing, and as it disappears over the horizon this mingles with a haunting oriental tune. Together and in harmony they fade away across the steppes.

Nocturne in D Major is one of Borodin's two string quartets. Sir Malcolm Sargent's orchestral arrangement of the slow movement, the highlight of the work, is extremely popular on my radio programme. This lush and melodious piece of music was the inspiration for the popular song 'This is My Beloved' from the successful musical *Kismet*. By this means the tune became well known to a very wide audience.

JOHANNES BRAHMS
(1833–1897)

Brahms was born into a poverty-stricken household in Hamburg. His father was a poorly paid musician and his mother, to help eke out the meagre family budget, was a seamstress. Yet from the beginning every effort was made to help Johannes satisfy his thirst for music. Formal music lessons began early and his advancement was swift. Before he turned fourteen he had made his concert début, but for several years he had to earn his living by giving lessons and playing in cheap saloons. At nineteen he was introduced to Eduard Reményi, a well-known Hungarian violinist, who was so impressed by the young man's ability that he engaged him as his accompanist. It was through Reményi that Brahms came to be interested in Hungarian folk music, which resulted later in the composition of his own Hungarian Dances.

Through his tours with Reményi he was able to meet some of the leading composers in Europe, including Schumann. When Brahms visited Schumann for the first time he was asked to play one of his own compositions. Schumann was astounded and called to his wife: 'Clara, you must hear this, such music as you've never heard before!' The Schumanns took Brahms to their hearts, and from that time their home was always open to him.

In the famous music journal edited by himself, Robert Schumann hailed Brahms in these words: 'Many new and remarkable talents have made their appearance even though their compositions are known only to a few. . . . There must, after such promise, suddenly appear one who will utter the highest ideal expression

40

of his time. . . . And he has come, this chosen youth. His name is Johannes Brahms.'

In 1862 Brahms decided to settle in Vienna where he stayed for the rest of his life. In the years following he began to write some of his most important music and his reputation grew steadily. His tremendous admiration for Beethoven's symphonies had seemingly discouraged him from attempting such a work. 'I shall never compose a symphony,' he said; 'you have no conception of how it feels to hear the tramp of a giant like Beethoven behind you.' When in fact, at the age of forty-three, he did compose his first symphony it was poorly received, and was even cynically referred to as 'the Beethoven tenth'. But between 1877 and 1884 he completed three other symphonies, and there is no doubt that his creative genius, in all forms of music except opera, proved him to be worthy of a place among the world's greatest composers.

In his last years he enjoyed the fame and security he had earned. He lived in modest fashion avoiding the public glare, while the whole world was ready to show him every honour.

Wiegenlied. When Brahms was twenty-five he formed the Hamburg Ladies' Choir. As a lone man in such a situation he not unexpectedly developed an attachment for one of the singers, a girl named Bertha. Though their close friendship ended when she returned home to Vienna they still communicated. She later married, and on the birth of her first child Brahms made her a present of a lullaby—the *Wiegenlied*, most famous of all his songs.

Variations on a Theme by Haydn in B Flat Major (*St Anthony Chorale*). Brahms discovered the theme, part of a divertimento for wind instruments, when he was asked to examine some Haydn manuscripts. Doubts have since arisen as to whether the theme was in fact of Haydn's own composition, or of unknown origin. In recent years it has been suggested that the theme, the *St Anthony Chorale*, could be an old pilgrim hymn. Brahms's set of symphonic variations on the theme was first played at a Vienna

Philharmonic concert in 1873. Brahms also arranged the work for two pianos.

German Requiem. For this, among the noblest of choral works, Brahms used his own text, drawing upon words from the Bible. But there are differences of opinion as to whether it was his mother's death that moved him to write the *Requiem* or, as had been mooted, he intended it to be 'the last funeral rite for Schumann'. Brahms allowed three of the movements to be presented in Vienna at the end of 1867, with a most unfortunate result. The performance was greeted by a disgraceful exhibition of booing and hissing that prompted Hanslick, the famous Austrian music critic, to call it 'a Requiem for the good manners of the Viennese public'.

But on Good Friday 1868, in Bremen Cathedral, with Brahms himself conducting, the full *Requiem* met with a magnificent reception. Of the seven movements, the one based upon the eighty-fourth Psalm, and known in English as 'How Lovely is Thy Dwelling Place', is the one most frequently heard.

Hungarian Dances. One of Brahms's great pleasures was to sit and listen to the Hungarian melodies of the gipsy fiddlers in the cafés of the Prater in Vienna. Often they would improvise their exciting music for him alone.

When he came to write his Hungarian Dances he at no time claimed them as original. In fact he called them 'arrangements'. Of the full twenty-one only two or three are said to be his own tunes, and when he sent the first group to his publisher, the accompanying letter said: 'I offer them as genuine gipsy children which I did not beget, but merely brought up with bread and milk.' They were piano duets, these 'gipsy children', and all of them were later arranged for orchestra by Brahms himself, Dvořák and others.

Alto Rhapsody was composed in 1869 during one of Brahms's sombre periods at the end of a love affair. The inspiration was a poem by Goethe called 'Journey through the Harz Mountains'. Full of anguish, the poem matched Brahms's own unhappy state.

The final section of the music is the most intensely beautiful part. Over the accompanying men's chorus the soloist expresses the hopes and faith of both the poet and the musician in the words that begin, 'But if from Thy Psalter, all-loving Father, one strain can but come to his hearing, O enlighten his heart'.

Piano Concerto no. 2 in B Flat. Brahms had composed a piano concerto some twenty years before this one, but it was not favourably received. The early sketches for the second concerto were made under the warm Italian sun during two trips to that country. It was completed in 1881 and first performed later that year in Budapest, with Brahms himself as the soloist. Now established, he could afford the dash of modesty he used when he referred to it as a 'tiny, tiny piano concerto'. But however he chose to regard it, the public saw it as large in stature, and from the outset it was warmly welcomed everywhere.

Of the four movements the *andante* is especially effective, opening with a 'cello solo of great beauty. Hints of two of Brahms's songs are interwoven with the melody, delicious ingredients of an impressive movement.

MAX BRUCH
(1838–1920)

To the music public at large, Bruch's name is instantly familiar by acquaintance with his frequently played Violin Concerto in G minor and, to a somewhat lesser extent, his piece for 'Cello and Orchestra, *Kol Nidrei*. But those who have studied his work contend that it is in his vast store of choral music that he was at his best, although this is almost unknown today.

As a boy, Bruch showed talent in two spheres; painting and music. By the time he was fourteen he had composed some seventy works, including a symphony which received a performance in his native city of Cologne. It seemed inevitable that music was to be his career.

Within ten years his name was known all over Germany, giving him a reputation that, in 1877, brought him an invitation to England. The outcome of the visit was that many of his choral and orchestral works were heard in this country for the first time, and three years later he was appointed conductor of the Liverpool Philharmonic Society, in succession to Sir Julius Benedict. Vaughan Williams was one of his pupils.

Concerto for Violin and Orchestra in G Minor was one of three violin concertos composed by Bruch, and yet this is the only one which retains the popularity that originally made it a standard work in the violin repertoire.

It was revised several times before it received its first formal presentation in 1868, principally on the advice of Joseph Joachim to whom it is dedicated. But it was nine years before London was to hear the concerto, when the great Spanish virtuoso Pablo Sarasate introduced it to a British audience. It has been described as 'a jewel', and the heartfelt main theme of the *adagio* 'one of the melodic glories of the nineteenth century'.

Kol Nidrei, a piece for 'Cello and Orchestra, is based on an ancient Hebrew melody. *Kol Nidrei* means 'All Vows' and is sung at the beginning of the service on the eve of the Day of Atonement. Grandson of a Lutheran clergyman, Bruch invested the prayer with a profound reverence.

While not altogether Hebraic in character, the variations that follow the statements of the main theme retain much of the feeling of the prayer.

FRÉDÉRIC CHOPIN
(1810–1849)

It might be said that what Beethoven was to the symphony and Schubert to song, Chopin was to the piano—he was sometimes called the 'Soul of the Pianoforte'.

'Tragic, romantic, lyric, sweet, dreamy and grand—all possible expressions are found in his compositions, and all are sung by him upon this instrument in perfect beauty.' So wrote the great pianist Anton Rubinstein.

Frédéric Chopin was born near Warsaw in Poland. His father was of French extraction and kept a private school where the boy received his early education. He first played the piano at a public concert when he was nine, and was soon composing. The first piece we know of is a Polonaise dated 1822. Among his earliest compositions to attract attention were the variations on 'La Ci darem la mano', the Mozart duet from *Don Giovanni*. Schumann welcomed it with 'Hats off gentlemen, a genius!'

All his biographers speak of Chopin's gentle and sensitive nature. Pale and sad, his good looks tinged with melancholy seem to have impressed everyone who knew him. At sixteen he was the favourite pupil of the director of the Warsaw Conservatory who recognized his strikingly original talent.

Not long after leaving the Conservatory he went to Vienna where he gave a number of concerts. The audiences had never heard such music. They were used to Liszt who stunned them with 'thundering cascades', but in Chopin's music they were listening to the 'murmurings of the waterfall or the sighing of the midnight wind'. Vienna greeted him with open arms and the critics described him as a 'master of the first rank', and 'one of the most remarkable meteors blazing on the musical horizon'. Despite this adulation he confessed to Liszt that 'I am not suited for concert giving; the public intimidate me. You have the force to overwhelm them.'

In 1831 he set out for Paris. When his visit was announced, his fame having gone before him, the curiosity of the Parisian music lovers was unbounded. His first concert at the Salle Pleyel drew the town. Chopin became the rage of Paris, sought after and fêted. Sir Charles Hallé, the conductor who gave his name to the famous orchestra, heard Chopin in Paris and said: 'He carried you with him into a dreamland in which you would have liked to have dwelt for ever.'

Here in Paris in 1837 began the most frequently discussed episode of his life, his relationship with the authoress George Sand. No two authorities agree as to its exact nature, and although he was happy at the beginning and for long intervals, he suffered cruelly towards the end of the ten years they were together. She wrote: 'Two natures, the one rich in exuberance, the other in its exclusiveness, could not really mingle, and a whole world separated them.' Nevertheless, Chopin was broken-hearted at their parting, and he told a friend that 'all the cords that bound me to life are broken'.

From that time, his health, which had always been poor, began to decline. Paris would never again be the same to him, and he was bent on leaving. He paid two visits to England, where, as in Paris, he was cordially received. But he was now a very sick man, and his loneliness eventually caused him to hurry back to Paris where he died soon after. He is buried between Cherubini and Bellini in the cemetery of Père Lachaise.

The Nocturnes. It is worth noting that the word 'nocturne' appears in the preface to the Prayer Book in connection with a service originally intended to be held at night. In musical terms it was first used by John Field (1782–1837), the Irish pianist and composer who invented the form to which Chopin added so much. Nowhere is Chopin's gift of melody shown to greater advantage than in these 'night pieces', compositions which, in their varying moods, have been called the 'tranquil musings of a lyric poet'. Amongst the best known are:

Opus 9 no. 2 in E Flat, the most famous of them all, which reminded one critic of Keats's 'Ode to a Nightingale'. It is supposed to have done more for Chopin's popularity in Paris than anything he had published hitherto. It is this piece that is some-times known as 'the' Chopin Nocturne.

Opus 15 no. 2 in F Sharp is surely one of the most beautiful. Its

46

main theme, tender and reflective, was compared thus to an oriental poem: 'It paints the palm and the cypress, and the great stars burning in the southern sky.'

Opus 27 no. 1 in C Sharp Minor is regarded by some as one of the high-points of Chopin's genius. It is probably the most dramatic of all the nocturnes, a work that has lent itself to much speculation as to its meaning, if in fact any was intended. One critic said melodramatically that it appeared to him to describe 'a calm night in Venice when, after a scene of murder, the sea closes over the corpse, while the moon shines serenely on'.

Opus 27 no. 2 in D Flat. I quote a Chopin pundit, who spoke of its 'lovely imploring melody. Nothing can equal its delicacy . . . a glow of gentle feeling lightly rippled with melancholy'.

The Études. It has often been emphasized that one should not be misled into thinking that Chopin composed these studies solely as exercises in the perfection of technique. They are more studies in melody, rhythm and emotional feeling, and their diversity of character is wide. In all there are twenty-seven études, two sets of twelve, the first of which is dedicated to 'My Friend, Franz Liszt'. Three others were published posthumously.

Opus 10 no. 3 in E. If we were to choose one étude as being more beautiful than any other, it would perhaps be this one, a delicious tone poem, more of a nocturne. Chopin himself declared that he had never written another such beautiful melody, 'The finest flowering of the composer's choice garden . . .'

Opus 10 no. 12 in C Minor is known as 'The Revolutionary Study'. It was written in 1831 under extreme emotional stress, when Chopin heard that Warsaw had fallen to the Russians. In this great dramatic outburst, he poured out his suffering and anxiety over the fate of his father and his family. Little more than a hundred years later, in 1939, it was the last piece of music broadcast on the Warsaw radio before the Germans overran the city, an act of defiance.

The Preludes, short pieces, sometimes mere sketches but each complete in itself, are among the most remarkable of Chopin's works. They express every shade of feeling. One writer aptly described them as 'the pearls of his music'. The two most often played are:

No. 6 in B Minor and no. 15 in D Flat Major. George Sand records an incident in Majorca when, after a heavy storm, she found Chopin seated at the piano playing the B Minor Prelude. The drops of rain falling on the roof seemed to her to be reflected in the music, but when she drew his attention to it, he denied that the piece was imitative in any way. On the contrary, Prelude no. 15 was the one nicknamed the 'Raindrop', apparently because of a notion that Chopin had elaborated the idea of the constantly falling raindrops that had been noticed in the sixth Prelude.

Sonata no. 2 in B Flat Minor is undoubtedly widely popular because of its third movement, the famous *Funeral March*, and a macabre story tells of how it came to be written, and since this is mentioned in a number of places, albeit in differing versions, we must accept that it contains some measure of truth.

Chopin, depressed as the result of a painful quarrel with George Sand, was attending a party at a friend's studio. Standing in a corner of the room was a human skeleton which had been acquired by his host who was a practical joker and somewhat eccentric. It was cause of much amusement to those present. But Chopin sat apart, rapt in misery and staring at the skeleton as though unable to take his eyes from it. Reaching out suddenly, he seized it, pressed it to him, and walked to the piano, where he sat down with the skeleton beside him. The studio was silent in an instant; an object meant as a joke had become a thing of horror. With his eyes closed Chopin started to play, slowly, deliberately, improvising on four deep, sombre notes. Before a roomful of stunned observers he composed the entire *Funeral March* within about half an hour, a threnody that could only have been written by a soul in torment.

Fantaisie Impromptu in C Sharp Minor occupies a very high place in the realm of classical 'pops', and is a very definite favourite with many lovers of piano music. Why Chopin withheld this during his lifetime is a question that has not been answered. It was composed in 1834 and remained unpublished for twenty-one years. One theory suggests that Chopin, always fastidious about the minutest detail of his compositions, was not satisfied with it. But the public since has disagreed in no uncertain manner.

Waltz in C Sharp Minor. A sense of sadness is discernible in this composition and, in the words of a writer on the music of Chopin, 'tender, lovesick longing cannot be depicted more sweetly nor entrancingly than in this waltz'. So beautifully represented by the waltz rhythm, its changing moods alternate time and again with those of the mazurka in an immaculate composition.

The *Military* Polonaise in A is the most famous of Chopin's twelve polonaises. Consistently bold and brilliant, he endeavoured in this glorious dance to convey some of the character of his native land. The name 'military' was not Chopin's. It doubtless arose because some perceived in its determined expression 'a clash of arms and the sound of stamping horses', a far cry from the dreamy reflective music which is usually attached to Chopin's name. This was one of Liszt's favourite pieces, and we are told that he played it at all his concerts.

JEREMIAH CLARKE
(1659–1707)

An English composer who was also prominent in his day as an organist, a position he occupied for a time at St Paul's Cathedral. The little we know about him is mainly concerned with the fact that he killed himself for the love of a lady.

He is remembered only as the composer of the celebrated *Trumpet Voluntary* which was originally attributed to Purcell. Called *The Prince of Denmark's March*, it was included in a 'A Choice Collection of Ayres for the Harpsichord' (1700). It was from this manuscript that Sir Henry Wood made his famous arrangement and gave it the title by which it is known today.

The Creed

The *Creed* is from the Second Liturgy of St John Chrysostom by the Russian composer Alexander Grechaninov (1864–1956). He was a pupil of Rimsky-Korsakov at the St Petersburg Conservatoire, and his works in various forms include five symphonies and many children's songs. He was considered to be 'the highest exponent of Russian composition, a master of choral orchestration', which is clearly evident in the *Creed*. The recording by the Choir of the Metropolitan Russian Church in Paris made it famous in this country.

'Crimond'

'Crimond'. On the main road between Peterhead and Fraserburgh lies the village of Crimond. It is the present church, built in 1812, that is associated with and in 1872 gave its name to this particular musical setting for the twenty-third Psalm. It is uncertain whether the melody, from the Scottish Psalter of 1650, was arranged by Jessie Irvine (the daughter of the Reverend Alexander Irvine, the minister of the church) or by David Grant of Aberdeen who might have named it 'Crimond' as a tribute to Jessie.

SIR WALFORD DAVIES

(1869–1941)

In 1934 he succeeded Elgar as Master of the King's Musick. His career as an organist included a long stay at the Temple Church in London, followed by an appointment at St George's Chapel, Windsor, and in the nineteen-thirties his name became widely known as an eminently successful broadcaster on music. As a composer he produced a substantial amount of choral music, little of which is heard today except for a fine setting of 'God be in my head', which is once again finding favour. His output included two symphonies and several oratorios, since forgotten. But apart from his official March for the Royal Air Force, his name is principally associated with the Solemn Melody, a piece for organ and strings composed in 1908 since when it has received the warm affection of the British public.

CLAUDE DEBUSSY

(1862–1918)

Debussy was one of the controversial figures of French music, deemed to be the initiator of the Impressionistic school and the oracle of 'the music of the future'.

He was born in Paris where he spent most of his life. His early studies were with a teacher who had been a pupil of Chopin, and his advance was so rapid that he was admitted to the Conservatoire by the age of eleven. Within a few years of his leaving, and having won the Prix de Rome, he began his rebellion against current musical dogma.

In Paris in the late eighties, Debussy mixed with many of those who were striving to develop new ideas in music, literature and art. Degas and Manet were among his friends, and he became absorbed in Manet's theories concerning colour, and the effects of light and atmosphere. These ideas took shape in his own mind as he became more clearly aware of the sort of music he wanted to write, music of fine and subtle texture.

He sought to reproduce in musical terms the misty shapes and beguiling effects of the Impressionist painters. His own palette became one of delicate orchestral tones. He was interested in sounds of nature: the 'sound' of silence, the rustling of the wind, the whispering of a gently flowing river. These were the voices he heard and incorporated in his music.

Prélude à l'Après-midi d'un faune ('Prelude to the Afternoon of a Faun') is a prelude composed in 1894 and first presented in Paris. In 1907 Debussy conducted the Queen's Hall Orchestra in a London performance. The prelude is based on a pastoral poem by Mallarmé in which a faun lies drowsing in the noonday sun. In his fancy he sees a vision of nymphs gambolling through the glade. When fully awake he recalls the scene again and again, asking himself was it real or only a dream? But sleep overtakes him and the question is never answered.

The work became the subject of a ballet devised by the Diaghilev company in Paris in 1912, with Nijinsky as principal dancer. Since then it has remained one of the most popular ballets in the repertoire.

Clair de lune is by far the most popular of the four pieces for piano that make up the *Suite Bergamasque*. Light and graceful, *Clair de lune* suggests the play of shifting moonbeams, and with its air of stillness and tranquillity, it is music most aptly described as 'atmospheric'

LÉO DELIBES

(1836–1891)

With such notable ballet scores as *Coppélia* and *Sylvia* to his credit (both composed about a hundred years ago), it is not surprising that Delibes has been called the father of modern ballet. He was certainly the first composer to treat music for the ballet seriously, and he undoubtedly exercised an influence on Tchaikovsky. Elgar once admitted that he too had come under the spell of this French composer.

Delibes, in his early manhood, earned his living as an organist, but he had always been attracted to the theatre. Several operettas of his had failed to gain any attention at all, and then, by dint of good fortune, he obtained the position of chorus master at the Paris Opéra. Not long after his arrival he was asked by the management to collaborate on a new ballet with the already established Polish composer Minkus. Delibes's contribution was just one act, but his music was so outstanding, and eclipsed that of his partner so completely, that his name was made overnight. His subsequent works only served to increase his fame and musical standing. He wrote some of the most delightfully scored ballet music of the nineteenth century.

No less graceful and melodious is his opera *Lakmé* which enjoys a perennial popularity in France.

Coppélia, subtitled 'The Girl with the Enamel Eyes', took its bow at the Paris Opéra in 1870. It was an immediate success with both audiences and critics. The Paris journals lavished praise on its 'distinguished, piquant and colourful score, excellently orchestrated'. With its charming setting of life in an Austrian village, it was the first of the ballets that used as its subject the story of a doll that comes to life. And with Swanhilda's Csárdás, it set the fashion of incorporating folk dances in ballet music. Its place in the world of ballet has been firmly held since that evening of 25 May 1870.

Sylvia, Le Pas des fleurs, was composed six years later, and though not quite so famous, I think perhaps that it has more memorable tunes than *Coppélia*—its Pizzicato is the most familiar of all Delibes's ballet music. The Intermezzo in Act I and the caressing solo violin of the *pas de deux* in Act III are among my fondest recollections of a ballet that is always affectionately welcomed at Covent Garden.

Lakmé. Although Delibes produced about twenty works for the opera house, he is thought of as a one-opera composer.

Presented first in 1883, Lakmé is based on an autobiographical novel by Pierre Loti, an extravagant story set in the India of the British Raj. The opera is known in this country only by the 'Bell Song', an aria of haunting beauty that has always been a soprano favourite for the opportunity it provides for *coloratura* singing. But there are also many tuneful moments throughout the duet 'Dôme Épais', for example, and there are passages of the most tender love music in this romantic opera which brims with languorous, sensuous melody.

Nor should one overlook the ballet music. The Hindu Dances evoke all the characteristically exotic colour of the Orient.

To hear the 'Bell Song' at its best, obtain, if you can, Joan Sutherland's very first recording of it in the two-record set called 'The Art of the Prima Donna'.

FREDERICK DELIUS

(1862–1934)

Much of Delius's music reminds me of the countryside seen through the haze of a summer afternoon. I listen, not always able to comprehend even after several hearings, and yet when it is over it has left an agreeable memory. The diffused quality of the music stays in the mind. Or am I thinking only of such pieces as 'On hearing the first cuckoo in Spring' or 'In a Summer Garden', to the latter of which Delius attached some lines that paint a lovely, simple picture? 'Roses, lilies and a thousand scented flowers. Bright butterflies flitting from petal to petal in the quivering summer air. . . .'

Bradford in Yorkshire can claim Delius as a native son. He declined to follow his father, who was of German origin, into the textile trade, and went instead to manage an orange plantation in Florida. It was there that he began to devote himself to music, and on returning to Europe he went to study at Leipzig. Here he met Grieg from whom he learnt a great deal. Two years later, in 1888, he moved to Paris where he began serious composition. He eventually settled in the small town of Grez-sur-Loing, near Fontainebleau, where he was to spend the rest of his life.

His early years were a struggle for recognition. His sensitive tone poems were not readily accepted in this country, and it was mainly due to the enthusiasm and persistence of Sir Thomas Beecham that his work was brought to the notice of British music lovers.

In 1922 Delius was beset by the direst adversity. An illness left him paralysed and three years later he became blind. He was only able to continue his music through the devoted and unstinting help of a young Yorkshire musician named Eric Fenby who, hearing of Delius's misfortunes, offered to serve him in any way he could. Fenby joined him in 1928, and stayed with the composer till the end. They devised a method by which Delius dictated his ideas to the young man and, in time, Fenby developed an almost uncanny ability to transmit those musical thoughts to paper.

'On hearing the first cuckoo in Spring', composed in 1912, is one of the most perfectly accomplished of Delius's sound pictures. It is based on a Norwegian folksong called 'In Old Valley', the words of which are rather gloomy, but he sensed in the melody an intimate beauty that effectively expressed his vision of spring. Much as we would like to think of this piece as a portrayal of the English countryside, the inspiration was probably Delius's love for the mountains of Norway.

'Brigg Fair', described by Delius as an 'English rhapsody', is a set of variations on a Lincolnshire folksong, which had been taken down by Percy Grainger while on a visit to that county. He passed it to Delius, and received the dedication in return. The composition delicately reflects the pastoral scene and the tale of a country love.

> *It was on the fifth of August,*
> *The weather fine and fair,*
> *Unto Brigg Fair I did repair*
> *For love I was inclined.*
>
> *I rose up with the morning lark*
> *My heart so full of glee,*
> *Of thinking there to meet my dear*
> *Long time I'd wished to see.*

'La Calinda', best known in the arrangement by Eric Fenby, comes from Delius's opera *Koanga*, which he composed early in his career. It is a dance played at the wedding festivities of two slaves on a plantation in Louisiana, and obviously a product of Delius's stay in the United States.

GAETANO DONIZETTI

(1797–1848)

Donizetti may well be considered the fastest opera composer in history. *Don Pasquale*, for example, was written in eleven days and *L'elisir d'amore* in a fortnight. 'Writing music,' Donizetti once stated, 'is nothing,' a boast he could prove by often composing a complete act of an opera in an evening.

The son of a weaver of Bergamo in Italy, Donizetti early showed unusual musical ability, and rather than study law as his father wished, he went his own way towards a career in music. His studies were interrupted, however, by a period of army service. While he was stationed in Venice three operas had come from his pen within a mere two years and, what is more, all received performances. From that time on one followed another in quick succession. In the course of thirty years he wrote sixty-five operas, though all but a few have passed into oblivion. Within his abundant talent he showed an equal facility for the tragic and the comic.

In 1844 he suffered a mental breakdown, and was an invalid for the remaining years of his life.

L'elisir d'amore ('The Elixir of Love'), a sparkling comic opera with a text by the celebrated librettist Romani, is one of the most pleasing that the Bergamo composer ever wrote. In a simple story of life in a Tuscan village, amusing situations are charmingly combined with the most delectable music.

Its best-known numbers include the famous tenor aria, 'Una furtiva lagrima', 'A furtive tear (glistens on her cheek)', one of the loveliest arias in all Italian opera and one of the most exceptional of Donizetti's inspirations.

'Quanto è bella', also for tenor, and the duet 'Venti Scudi', are other highlights in a score that has captivated audiences the world over.

Lucia di Lammermoor is generally conceded to be Donizetti's masterwork. Based on Sir Walter Scott's novel *The Bride of Lammermoor*, the opera was first produced at the Teatro San Carlo, Naples, in 1835. Another opera based on the same story had been presented in Padua a year before by a little-known composer, but it was so overwhelmed by Donizetti's version that it sank without trace.

Set in Scotland in 1700, the story tells of the tragic fate of a pair of lovers torn apart by family strife. Two numbers in particular have contributed to the opera's lasting fame.

The sextet at the end of the second act has been described by Kobbé as one of the finest pieces of dramatic music in all opera, rivalled only by the quartet in *Rigoletto*. He mentions that he was present at Caruso's first appearance in this opera at the Metropolitan in New York. The reception given to the sextet was so vociferous that the police, thinking a disturbance had broken out, entered the auditorium ready to quell a riot.

The opera's other famous number is the 'Mad Scene', which takes place during Lucia's wedding celebrations. Distracted through being forced to marry against her will, in the madness that overcomes her she kills her bridegroom. Appearing before the assembled guests, Lucia reveals her agony in a heartrending aria at the end of which she herself falls dying. By any reckoning this is a *tour de force* for *coloratura* sopranos, and celebrated Lucias have numbered among them Melba, Tetrazzini, Galli-Curci and, in our own generation, Joan Sutherland.

Don Pasquale, in its rare sprightliness and elegance, is the very essence of true *opera buffa*. The unabashed absurdity of the plot is blended with music that matches every delicious moment of its gay comedy. The score includes such gems as the famous tenor serenade, 'Com é gentil', said to be a last-minute addition without even an accompaniment written for it, the duet 'Tornami a dir', and the chorus in Act III in which the servants forgather to comment in whispers on the goings-on in the household.

'Don't be cross'

'Don't be cross' ('Sei nicht bös'). This song comes from the operetta *Der Obersteiger* ('The Master Miner') by Carl Zeller (1842–98). Though music was not his full-time occupation (he was an official in the Austrian ministry of education), he became one of the most popular operetta composers of his time, his biggest success being *Der Vogelhändler* ('The Bird Seller'). 'Don't be cross' is about a miller's daughter who is wooed by a young fisherman. Thinking she can improve her status in life she rejects him, saying 'Don't be cross, it cannot be'. When she returns later, disillusioned with her experience of the outside world, she asks the fisherman to comfort her—only to be paid back in her own coin.

ANTONIN DVOŘÁK
(1841–1904)

Dvořák was born of humble stock in a small town near Prague in what was then Bohemia and is now Czechoslovakia. His father, an innkeeper of small means, would have preferred his son to become a butcher.

Dvořák took his first music lessons from his schoolmaster, and at sixteen was sent to the organ school at Prague. For several years he endured intense poverty, and was reduced to playing the viola in the streets to help keep body and soul together. When he graduated he was able to secure the interest of Smetana, who obtained a position for him at the National Theatre, where he made a precarious living.

During the next ten years, according to Dvořák, 'I studied

with God, with the birds, with the trees, the rivers and myself'. His earliest composition to attract attention was a *Hymnus* for mixed choir and orchestra, and two years later his Symphony in E Flat won him the Austrian State Prize. But he first savoured real success with the appearance of his Slavonic Dances in 1878. From this beginning Dvořák's fame was to spread throughout Europe. His music also enjoyed wide popularity in England. His cantata, 'The Spectre's Bride', was written specially for the Birmingham Festival, and he was honoured by Cambridge University. By this time he was one of the world's leading composers.

In 1892 he was invited to become the director of the National Conservatory of Music in New York. He spent three years in America, during which time he composed his most celebrated work, the Symphony *From The New World*. When he returned to Prague it was as head of the Conservatory there, a post he occupied from 1901 till the end of his life. He is regarded now as his country's greatest composer, and it was said of him that 'his music was best when it smacked of the soil and the dances dear to his own people'.

Symphony no. 9 in E Minor, *From The New World*, one of the best loved of all symphonies, was first performed by the New York Philharmonic Orchestra in 1893. Anton Seidl who conducted it declared that 'it is not a good name, "New World". It is homesickness, yearning,' and he insisted that the work was essentially Bohemian. For years the symphony was the subject of controversy, concerned chiefly with whether or not Dvořák had borrowed American Negro folk tunes, particularly in the second movement, the famous *largo*. There was even the astonishing suggestion that this movement was inspired by the story of Hiawatha in Longfellow's poem, and that one of the passages in the music depicted Minnehaha sobbing as she bade Hiawatha farewell. Dvořák denied that his tunes or his thoughts were anything but original. The argument has long been forgotten and the symphony accepted as a tribute to his host country; his homage, as a stranger, to his friends in a foreign land.

Symphony no. 8 in G Major. Of Dvořák's nine symphonies and apart from *The New World*, only one or two others are played at all. Of these, the lighthearted G Major symphony—sometimes referred to as the *English* Symphony because it was first published in London—still retains its popularity. It was conducted by Dvořák himself when it was first introduced to the British audience in 1890. The *Musical Times* said afterwards that 'it was like the Pastoral Symphony, having been written under the influence of country sights and sounds; all is fresh and charming'. The third movement, a graceful *allegretto*, is often requested in my programme.

Slavonic Dances. The impecunious Dvořák experienced a stroke of good fortune through his friendship with Brahms, who introduced him to his own publisher in a letter containing these words: 'I took much pleasure in the works of Dvořák of Prague. Decidedly he is a very talented man. Besides, he is poor. Please take this into consideration.' On the strength of this, Dvořák was commissioned to write some Slavonic Dances in the manner of Brahms's Hungarian Dances. He produced a set of four-handed piano pieces that proved so popular he was asked to orchestrate them, in which versions they are now best known. A second set appeared eight years later and met with equal success.

Russalka, Dvořák's fairy-tale opera, contains pages of delightful 'elfin' music. It is known to British listeners by one aria of great beauty, 'O Silver Moon'. The opera itself is based on a Slavonic folk legend about a water sprite.

'*Songs my mother taught me*'. Among Dvořák's songs—and there are fifty or so of them—this stands out, not only because of its appealing sentiment, but also because it is a perfect piece of writing. It comes from a group of Gipsy Songs composed in

1880, which tell of the sorrows of a freedom-loving, wandering race. The words are derived from folk origins, and the tune is based on a traditional gipsy air.

EDWARD ELGAR

(1857–1934)

Elgar was largely self-taught. His father was a church organist and music dealer with a shop in Worcester. As might be expected, the conversation the young Elgar heard at home was nearly always of a musical nature.

It was not long before he availed himself of the opportunities that were open to him in such an environment. As his interest in music grew, he began to teach himself as many instruments as he could, and he became a pianist, acquiring quite a reputation in the district as an accompanist. He also played the organ rather well, and when his father retired he took his place at the church services.

He tried his hand at most things in the way of music. When he was about twenty-two he became the bandmaster at the County Asylum, with the staff as musicians. But the violin was to be his chief instrument, and he played it professionally in various orchestras. Hoping to further himself he went to London, but the distractions of the big city were not to his liking, and he returned to his native county and the more peaceful setting of Malvern.

It was several years before he produced his first composition to make an impact. 'Scenes from the Saga of King Olaf' was presented in 1896 at the North Staffordshire Festival at Hanley. From this moment Elgar's career went from strength to strength. With the *Enigma* Variations in 1899, and *The Dream of Gerontius* a year later (although it was poorly received at its first performance), he established himself as this country's finest composer. Such had become the interest in his music that in 1903 an Elgar Festival was held at Covent Garden. The following year he received a knighthood.

The death of his wife in 1920 so affected him that for nine years he wrote nothing at all. It was a period of silence to be broken only when, as Master of the King's Musick, he composed a prayer for the recovery of King George V who was seriously ill.

Elgar was often accused of pandering to the taste of the 'man in the street', particularly in his marches and such pieces as the Overture *Cockaigne*. To this he replied: 'For my part, I know there are a lot of people who like to celebrate events with music. To these people I have given tunes. Is that wrong? Why should I write a fugue or something that won't appeal to anyone, when the people yearn for things which can stir them?' He wrote from the heart, and believed in everything he wrote.

Variations on an Original Theme: The *Enigma* Variations. To each of these Elgar appended initials or a pseudonym that puzzled the world of music for years after the first performance in 1899. Musicologists attempted to decipher the cryptic markings that hid the identity of the personalities represented, and all Elgar would say was: 'In this music I have sketched, for their amusement and mine, the idiosyncrasies of thirteen of my friends. . . . The variations should stand simply as a piece of music, the enigma I will not explain. Its dark saying must be left unguessed.' Only after Elgar's death were the facts of the matter revealed.

The ninth variation, marked 'Nimrod', is the best known of them all and often played on its own. It is the musical portrait of A. J. Jaeger, then a member of the firm of Novello, the music publishers, to whom the manuscript was first shown. *Jaeger* is German for 'hunter', and the Bible says that Nimrod was a mighty hunter. The fourteenth and final variation stands for Elgar himself.

Dream of Gerontius. This great oratorio, based on a poem by Cardinal Newman, did much to enhance Elgar's name and reputation. But not as a result of its introduction to the public at the Birmingham Festival of 1900. It was a disastrous performance from every point of view. Rehearsals, interrupted by illness and other causes, developed into a shambles, and the work was far from ready to be heard, although it was given the place of honour and the famous Hans Richter conducted. The principal singers were Edward Lloyd, Plunket Greene and Marie Brema, a noted dramatic soprano. Vaughan Williams was present to comment that 'Plunket Greene lost his voice, and Miss Brema had none to lose!' No wonder that first audience gave the work such a poor reception, while in Germany it was accepted as a masterpiece. In England it had to wait two years before it was given another chance to prove itself, at the Three Choirs Festival in 1902.

Pomp and Circumstance March no. 1 in D Major. Elgar had originally planned a series of six military marches under this title, which is a quotation from Act III of Shakespeare's *Othello*, but only five were completed. No. 1 was first played at a concert given by the Liverpool Philharmonic Society in October 1901. Later that year, this and no. 2 were performed at a Promenade Concert at the Queen's Hall in London. Sir Henry Wood, in *My Life in Music*, wrote: 'I shall never forget the scene at the end of the first of them—the one in D Major. The people simply rose and yelled. I had to play it again—with the same result; in fact they refused to let me go on with the programme. . . . Merely to restore order, I played the march a third time. . . . Little did I think then that the lovely broad melody of the trio would one day develop into our second national anthem—"Land of Hope and Glory".'

Elgar was well aware, as he said, that he had a tune 'that would knock them flat'. It is thought to have been Edward VII who suggested that the tune should be made into a song. With the now immortal words by A. C. Benson, it became the choral finale of the *Coronation Ode*.

Introduction and Allegro for Strings dates from 1905. The idea for the composition had occurred to Elgar on a visit to Cardiganshire several years earlier. In his own words, 'On the cliff between blue sea and blue sky there came up to me the sound of singing. The songs were too far to reach me distinctly, but one point in common to all impressed me, from which I made the tune which appears in the Introduction. Though there may be, and I hope there is, a Welsh feeling in this one theme, the work really is a tribute to that sweet borderland where I have made my home.'

Violin Concerto in B Minor. Elgar dedicated this to Fritz Kreisler, the concerto's first soloist at a Philharmonic Society concert in 1910 at which the composer himself was conducting. The work contains some of the loveliest music that ever came from his pen, and his genius for lyrical writing is revealed in the slow movement, an *andante* that goes straight to the heart of the listener.

Salut d'Amour and *Chanson de Matin* are two of Elgar's smaller pieces, both regarded with great affection.

Salut d'Amour is one of his earliest compositions and was originally entitled 'Liebesgruss', which literally translated means 'Love's Greeting'. It was given its present name because the publisher thought it would have more appeal if this were in French. It was written for Elgar's daughter Clarice.

Chanson de Matin is one of two pieces (the other being *Chanson de Nuit*) written for violin and piano and later arranged for small orchestra by W. H. Reed. They were first given at the same Promenade Concert which introduced the *Pomp and Circumstance* March no. 1 to London. *Chanson de Matin* was judged 'blithe and dewy-eyed', a compliment that has been echoed by audiences for over seventy years.

'Elizabethan Serenade'

A firm favourite written by Ronald Binge, an English composer who has many light orchestral works to his credit, and whose chief concern is with music for films and television.

'The Fairy Song'

'The Fairy Song' from *The Immortal Hour*. This song, 'How beautiful they are, the lordly ones', is the only remembered music from *The Immortal Hour*, an opera based on a play and Celtic poems by Fiona Macleod, the pen-name of William Sharp. The composer was Rutland Boughton (1878–1960), who attempted to found at Glastonbury an English equivalent of Bayreuth to produce music dramas on the legends of King Arthur. After three productions the scheme failed, but *The Immortal Hour*, a less ambitious presentation, was the one success and his company, the Festival Players, brought it to London in 1922, where it enjoyed a long run at the Regent Theatre, King's Cross.

GABRIEL FAURÉ

(1845–1924)

Though he composed a great deal, Fauré's music has never been very widely known or popular in the sense of mass appeal. He is regarded principally as a writer of songs, and indeed one critic referred to him as the 'French Schubert'. His orchestral suite *Pelléas et Mélisande*, from the incidental music to Maeterlinck's play, first given in English by Mrs Patrick Campbell in 1898, is still sometimes heard at concerts. But to the average music-lover in this country Fauré is best known by two works.

Pavane, a sensitive and tuneful composition, is virtually based on a single theme, stated first by a most attractive flute solo. It has, in several instances, been used as accompaniment to a ballet.

Fauré's *Requiem* is one of the most profoundly moving choral works of our day, introduced at the Church of the Madeleine in Paris in 1887, where Fauré himself was an organist. The *Requiem* was composed in memory of his father. Because it contains three sections which are not, in fact, part of the Mass for the Dead, and because of its musical form, it is not considered strictly liturgical. For this reason, permission had to be obtained before it could be performed at Fauré's own funeral.

FRIEDRICH FLOTOW

(1812–1883)

A German composer of eighteen operas only one of which is heard today, and that because of a single song which oddly enough was not of his original composition.

Martha, set in the England of Queen Anne, was unsuccessful under its original title of *Lady Harriet*. It was revised in 1847 and brought out in Vienna under its new title, including this time 'The Last Rose of Summer' which became famous the world over. The song had been known long before as one of Thomas Moore's Irish Melodies; Moore wrote both the words and the music. Some say that the melody is even older, and was called 'The Groves of Blarney'.

The opera has one other favourite number, the tenor aria usually known by its Italian title 'M'appari'.

CÉSAR FRANCK
(1822–1890)

It was said of this modest little man with the bushy side-whiskers and ill-fitting clothes that 'He seemed to be surrounded by music as by a halo'. If you happened upon him walking in the streets of Paris, talking and gesticulating to himself—which was often quite startling to passers-by—he would be the last person you would take to be the centre of a vehement musical controversy. The inoffensive César Franck, organist of the church of Ste Clotilde, was probably on his way to give a piano lesson to some pupil or other in order to augment a very meagre income.

He was born in Liège, and from his very early years was the victim of a father who was over-ambitious for his son's advancement and ever-ready to exploit the boy as a virtuoso. At eleven he was taken on a tour of Belgium, giving concerts in almost every town. In 1848 when his studies were over he married a young actress. This was during the French Revolution and Franck recalled that, to get to the church, he and his bride had to climb the barricades and convince the armed guards of their purpose. One of the fortunate aspects of his marriage was that he escaped from his father's household and its smothering influence.

For many years afterwards he suffered disappointment. His works that did reach the concert hall were often badly performed, due mainly to the derogatory attitude of the musicians who cared little for his music, which they considered unorthodox. Franck was a creator in advance of his time.

His Symphonic Variations for piano and orchestra met with disapproval, and yet are accepted by soloists now as rewarding to play. Franck was sixty-seven when his D Minor Symphony was grudgingly performed by the orchestra of the Paris Conservatoire. The musicians were uninterested, the audience perplexed and the experts raised their hands in horror. It was not until the last year of his life that he could say: 'The public is beginning to understand me.'

Among the few occasions during his lifetime when an audience greeted his music with any warmth was in 1882, when he conducted an early Mass of his to which the *Panis Angelicus* had been added at the last minute. Without exception this was considered the most beautiful part of the work. It was received enthusiastically and even encored, since when it has usually been sung separately at concerts and has become popular as a sacred song.

ALEXANDER GLAZUNOV
(1865–1936)

Glazunov became known as the 'Russian Mendelssohn'. One of the ablest of the nationalist group of Russian composers, he revealed an exceptional talent in his very early years. At fifteen he continued his studies with Rimsky-Korsakov who informed his pupil, at the end of a year and a half, that there was nothing more he could teach him. Glazunov was now an accomplished composer. Within twelve months he had written his first symphony, which was performed in St Petersburg and very well received. Three years later Liszt conducted it at Weimar. This was the beginning of an esteem that would spread well beyond the borders of his own country.

He became a prolific composer of music covering a wide field. In the course of time he produced eight symphonies (which, one must add, are rarely heard outside Russia today), a popular Violin Concerto, a large quantity of chamber music, ballets and orchestral suites, all of a quality that assured him an eminent place in Russian music. Though honoured by the Soviets, in 1928 he chose to settle in Paris where he spent his remaining days.

The Violin Concerto in A Minor came before the public for the first time at the Queen's Hall, London, in 1905. Sir Henry Wood was the conductor, and the soloist Mischa Elman. A notice of the occasion in the *Musical Times* said that 'the concerto was dedicated to Leopold Auer—one of the most famous violinists of the time—who had agreed to introduce it. Glazunov was visiting Auer while he was giving Mischa Elman a lesson, and was so impressed by the pupil's extraordinary ability that he asked Auer if he would allow Elman to give the first performance of the work, a request to which the distinguished violinist willingly assented'.

The Seasons is a ballet whose music describes the four seasons of the year. The favourite sections of the work are probably *Autumn*, to which Pavlova used to dance, and *Summer*, which pictures a field of corn swaying in the warm breeze. Cornflowers and poppies appear and dance to a beautiful waltz, an outstanding number in a very pleasing score.

CHRISTOPH WILLIBALD GLUCK
(1714–1787)

The inscription on his tombstone reads, 'Here lies an upright German man. A zealous Christian. A faithful spouse. Christoph Willibald Ritter von Gluck; Of the noble Art of Music a Great Master.' An epitaph as near perfect as you could wish, although not everyone agreed that the final statement was entirely the truth. As a rival once said of him, 'the famous Gluck may puff his own compositions but he cannot prevent them from boring us to death'. There were not in fact many dissenters to the view that Gluck was indeed a great master. He was the founder of modern opera, and Berlioz, for example, believed that 'the beautiful pages of Gluck will for ever remain beautiful'.

The son of a gamekeeper in the service of a prince of Bavaria, Gluck had a musical training that was varied and comprehensive from the first. The prince, who took a kindly interest in his game-keeper's son, persuaded the young man to accompany him to Italy where Gluck became a pupil of the well-known composer Giovanni Battistia Sammartini in Milan.

Once his studies were over, Gluck began to pour forth Italian operas to Italian audiences. In three years he had produced eight, all of which met with some success. His fame reached as far as London, and he was summoned by the management of the Haymarket Theatre to be their resident composer, ostensibly to create opposition to Handel who was then the reigning power. In London he met the great Mr Handel himself who, after listening to one of his operas, merely observed that Gluck 'knew no more of counterpoint than his cook', a remark hardly appreciated by the young composer who had worshipped Handel's very name and kept a large portrait of him in his bedroom. 'I want to see him when I open my eyes,' he said, 'and I want to look upon him with reverence and awe.'

Thus it was from Handel that Gluck received the first blow that was to lead him to reassess his work; his Italian operas had not pleased his English audiences. In 1748 he left hastily for Vienna, where for ten years he was the director of the Court Opera. It was during this period that he endeavoured to develop new ideas and to create a new style of opera. In 1762 came a fortunate meeting with the man who was to prove the perfect collaborator, and who provided him with a libretto after his own heart. That man was Ranierida Calzabigi, the writer of *Orpheus and Eurydice*.

But owing to the antagonism of the 'old school', Gluck was not altogether able to win over the Viennese audiences. Later in Paris too he had to overcome the same prejudice, and even with the support of Marie Antoinette, he met with intrigue, and when he presented his first French opera, *Iphigenia in Aulis*, he was attacked on all sides. Despite all this, an abbé who was one of the leaders of musical opinion in Paris at the time admitted that 'with such music one might found a new religion'. In the end Gluck triumphed, and the French were pleased to call him the 'Hercules of music'.

In all he composed some sixty operas, and in 1780 he returned to spend his last years in Vienna. He had amassed considerable wealth, and yet his old age does not appear to have been a happy one. By that time he was a sick man, often to be seen sitting in a box applauding the new symphonies by a young man called Mozart.

His doctor had forbidden him stimulants of any kind. But Gluck had always been fond of wine, and at a time when his system was least able to bear it, he craved for something more potent. His wife, ever watchful, succeeded in keeping alcohol from him for weeks at a time, but one evening he procured a bottle of brandy, and before she could stop him he had drained the contents. He died that night aged seventy-three. Not long before this he had received a visit from his friend and fellow composer Salieri, who informed him that he was writing a new religious work, and that he was undecided as to whether the role of Christ should be given to a baritone or a tenor. 'Don't worry,' said Gluck, 'very soon I shall be meeting our Saviour and I'll let you know!'

Orpheus and Eurydice. Of Gluck's four works that still hold the stage of the world's opera houses, the one that finds a particular place in my own programme is *Orpheus and Eurydice*, largely, I would say, because of Kathleen Ferrier's poignant recording of the opera's most famous aria in the third act, 'Che Faro . . .' ('What is life to me without thee'). Other popular passages include the 'Dance of the Blessed Spirits' which occurs in the second act, in the transition from the dark of Hades to the sunny skies of the Elysian Fields where the good spirits find rest. This serenity is exquisitely expressed in the slow dance with the famous flute solo. Also worthy of mention is 'Che puro Ciel' ('What pure light'), a tender aria with oboe obbligato that speaks of the joys of Elysium.

Henry Chorley, the noted English critic of the last century, wrote: 'There is no other opera in the world's long list which with merely three female voices and a chorus can return to the stage in days like ours to make the heart throb and the eyes water.'

CHARLES GOUNOD
(1818–1893)

Despite current opinion, there is no doubt that in his time and for years after Gounod was looked upon as a genius. He was born in Paris. His father, a painter of some repute, died when he was five and it was his mother, a gifted pianist, who gave the boy his first music lessons. He soon showed that he possessed a natural musical instinct and made rapid progress. For one thing, he had perfect pitch and would often amuse himself and his friends by trying to identify the key in which the dogs in the street were barking. At eighteen, his schooling over, he enrolled at the Paris Conservatoire where he made his mark by winning the Prix de Rome, which gave him three years' study in Italy. This played a significant part in shaping the trend of his whole life. He became interested in religious music in Rome, studying the works of the great Italian church composers, and regularly attending services in the Sistine Chapel. Moreover, he had made the acquaintance of a Dominican preacher, who, it appears, fired him with a zeal for a religious life.

When he returned to Paris in 1842 he secured the post of organist and precentor at a small mission church. This day-to-day contact with the ministry resulted in an intense desire to read for the priesthood. He entered the seminary of St Sulpice, and for two years wore the garb of a cleric. During this time one of his compositions was published as by the Abbé Gounod. Though he left to re-enter the lay world long before he had completed his theological studies, he remained a deeply religious man all his life.

In the years following his seclusion Gounod was far from idle, and his music was constantly before the public. A Mass in G Major appeared, and he produced several operas of which *Sappho* in particular was highly praised. The critics found it tuneful and recognized in it his gift for lyricism. Gounod was beginning to assert himself as one of France's outstanding composers.

In 1855 he presented his most famous religious work, the *Ste*

Cecilia Mass, and there was little doubt of his growing stature. Four years later came one of the real high points in Gounod's life, the production of *Faust*, and although it was not at first successful, it was in fact to be recognized as the fullest fruition of his remarkable talent.

There is an oft-told story that when he had reached his threescore years, he happened to be remarking on his great love for the music of Mozart. He confessed that 'when I was twenty, I just said "I". At thirty I said "I and Mozart". At forty, "Mozart and I", and now at sixty I say to myself, "Mozart"!'

When the Franco-Prussian war broke out in 1870, Gounod sought refuge in England where he was now well known. The atmosphere of Victorian Britain and its love of choral and sacred music suited him admirably. He was in his element here, and became a leading figure in musical circles. He founded the Albert Hall Choir, to be known later as the Royal Choral Society. He stayed five years and, when he went back to Paris, devoted himself almost entirely to the composition of religious works, the most prominent being the oratorios *Redemption* and *Mors et Vita*, both of which, except for one or two numbers, have fallen completely out of favour. In view of this, it is strange now to recall the words of Saint-Saëns' tribute to him: 'When in the distant future the operas of Gounod will have entered the dusty sanctuary of libraries known only to students, the *Redemption* and *Mors et Vita* will remain alive and will teach future generations what a musician France could boast in the nineteenth century.'

On 17 October 1893 Charles Gounod was dead. His wife entered his study to find his lifeless body slumped over his desk. He had been at work on a *Requiem* in memory of one of his grandchildren who had recently died.

Faust's first production in Paris in March 1859 met with no success, although parts of it were singled out for praise. Despite its failure, an enterprising publisher decided to take a chance and issue the score, and to his utter surprise it made him a fortune. Consequently, when *Faust* was reintroduced ten years later its success was assured, and to this day it has remained one of the best loved of all operas. Much of it is well known.

The Waltz, which is the finale of the second act, is familiar the world over. It is not really one waltz but four, each following the other in sweeping elegance.

'Salut, demeure', the tenor cavatina, is known in English as 'All hail, thou dwelling pure and lowly', a tender sentimental song.

The 'Jewel Song', Marguerite's aria when she discovers the casket, has been described as a 'Valse brillante and truly a gem'.

The 'Soldiers' Chorus' is another universally known tune: the soldiers return from war singing their rousing song 'Gloire Immortelle' ('Glory immortal').

In the final trio, 'Anges purs! Anges radieux!' ('Angels pure, radiant, bright!'), Marguerite in a soaring melody calls upon the angels to save her.

The ballet music. The tradition of the Paris Opera, at which *Faust* was produced again, required that a ballet be included. The librettists chose as their subject the Walpurgis Night revels—the eve of May Day—at which Faust meets the courtesans of antiquity. The ballet consists of seven numbers, and is in fact frequently omitted when the opera is produced today.

'Ave Maria' (Bach and Gounod). Gounod wrote nine Masses and much other sacred music besides. But of all his religious compositions the one which has attained the greatest popularity is this 'Ave Maria' for soprano. It is in fact the first Prelude in C Major of Bach's *Well-Tempered Clavier* over which Gounod wrote a melody called *Meditation*.

Messe Solennelle à Ste Cécile is the first part of a trilogy regarded by Gounod as the centre of all his religious music. It was dedicated to his father-in-law who had died in 1853, but not until two years later was the Mass performed for the first time at the Church of St Eustace in Paris. The other parts of the trilogy are:

The oratorio *Redemption*, for which Gounod's earliest sketches were made in 1860. It was not completed until 1881. He wrote the text himself and dedicated the work to Queen Victoria. It had its initial performance at the Birmingham Festival of 1882, and was given in Paris for the first time two years later, at a concert conducted by Widor. The one chorus still heard today is 'Unfold ye Portals'.

Mors et Vita is a cantata dedicated to Pope Leo XIII, and it was Gounod once again who supplied the words. The Birmingham Festival was once more chosen for the première of his work, in 1884. As with the other parts of the trilogy, it was a resounding success. Nowadays the orchestral interlude *Judex* is the only reminder of its erstwhile, world-wide fame. Gounod said that he had attempted to treat the music in the style of 'fresco', as religious paintings. In this connection, when Franceschi, the sculptor and painter and then director of the French Academy in Rome, first heard the cantata, he was so impressed that he sent the composer a picture of a corner of the Sistine Chapel, and inscribed the gift 'To my dear musician Gounod from Michelangelo'.

EDVARD GRIEG

(1843–1907)

Grieg is sometimes referred to as the 'Chopin of the North', which is not to gainsay that he had an individuality of his own. His career was at one time summed up thus: 'The voice is the voice of Grieg. He wears no man's mantle—and borrows no man's speech.'

Grieg came from Bergen in Norway and his ancestors were immigrants from Scotland. One of five children, he was brought up in a home where there had always been a deep interest in music. His first faltering attempts at the piano were taken in hand by his mother when he was six, and he later remarked that he was completely overawed by her cleverness, and that his talent for music came from her.

While still at school Grieg composed a set of piano variations that greatly impressed the famous Norwegian violinist, Ole Bull, who advised him to go to Leipzig and become a musician. This he did, at the age of fifteen. He stayed for four years, and confessed some time later that he left the conservatory as stupid as he had come to it. Nevertheless, his early piano pieces and songs were already showing technical skill of a high quality. It was Grieg's songs to words by Hans Christian Andersen that made his name known in the Scandinavian countries, and within a short time his Sonata in F for Violin and Piano had further enhanced his reputation.

There now began a period in his life in which he felt he was suffocating within the narrow confines of his surroundings. He was actively composing and organizing concerts but, unhappily, frustration met him at every point. For some reason malice and petty intrigue were getting him down, and he realized that if only for a while the time had come for him to go away. Money was short, and his intention was to apply to the government for an allowance so that he could travel abroad.

At this point Grieg wrote to a friend: 'One day in December 1868, when everything seemed dark, I received a letter from Liszt which brought sunlight into my universe. There was at that time no one in my country who cared anything at all about me as a creative artist. I had expressed my despondent feelings in a letter to a Roman friend. He had spoken of it to Liszt (now living in Rome) whom he knew was warmly interested in me; and it shows a very noble trait in Liszt that he sat down immediately at his writing table, conscious of the good that he could thereby accomplish. I had thought it worth while to apply for a travelling stipend, but had little hope of getting one since I was in the black books of our conservative musicians, and the rest of the ruling music dilettantes.' Liszt's letter worked wonders. It was such that when Grieg enclosed it with his application for an allowance, it was readily granted.

His meetings with Liszt had been, for him, of the greatest importance. When Grieg showed him several of his compositions and Liszt played them over, expressing enthusiasm for them, Grieg considered his journey had been a triumph. This was the turning point in his career. He returned home with renewed confidence and belief in his future. Many of the ideas he had been storing and the sketches he had made for future works were now ready to be released in full measure. In the years following he produced some of his most famous compositions, including the *Peer Gynt* music, and his piano concerto was given its first public hearing.

Steadily, his music was becoming known and appreciated

77

throughout Europe. When he appeared as pianist or conductor he was greeted with extraordinary fervour, signs that he was achieving a popularity enjoyed by few musicians of his time. His home 'Troldhaugen', in the countryside near Bergen, was a mecca for music lovers who came to pay him homage. He spent thirty years of his life here, the last of them in sickness. On 4 September 1907 he died peacefully in his sleep. His ashes rest in a grotto in a wall at 'Troldhaugen', looking towards a fjord he greatly loved.

Concerto for Piano and Orchestra in A Minor. This was written in the summer of 1868 when Grieg was twenty-five. It was a happy time for him, as he had been married for a year and his daughter had just been born. This beautiful concerto was seen as an expression of joy from the fullness of his heart.

It was introduced on 3 April 1869, in Copenhagen. Edmund Neupart, the soloist, wrote to Grieg after the performance: 'On Saturday your divine concerto resounded in the great hall of the Casino. The triumph I achieved was tremendous. Even as early as the cadenza in the first movement the public broke into a real storm. The three dangerous critics, Gade, Rubinstein and Hartmann, sat in the stalls and applauded with all their might. I am to send you greetings from Rubinstein and say that he is astounded to have heard a composition of such genius. He would like to make your acquaintance.'

This, one of the most popular of all piano concertos, is rich in choice and striking themes with constant reminders of the Norwegian folk melodies to which Grieg had always been attracted.

Peer Gynt Suites. Henrik Ibsen, the celebrated Norwegian dramatist, wrote to Grieg in 1874, asking if he would supply the incidental music to a drama he was contemplating. The play tells of a wild, impetuous peasant lad who wanders the face of the earth, a prey to morbid dreams of adventure. The first performance, in Christiana (now Oslo) in February 1876, was most successful. Some of the exquisitely beautiful music was later arranged by the composer in two suites, the first of which is in four sections:

Morning is expressive of the mountain scenery at the rising of the sun. Peer Gynt looks out upon the world.

Aase's Death is a tragic piece of music considered by Grieg to be among his best work.

Anitra's Dance, with its hint of the Orient, is the music that accompanies the dance of Anitra, the daughter of a Bedouin chief in whose tent Peer Gynt is being entertained.

In the Hall of the Mountain King is a vivid description of the wild antics of the little people, the Trolls, in their mountain haunt.

The best known item in the Second Suite is *Solveig's Song*, based on a Norwegian folk air. After great wanderings, Peer Gynt returns home, now an old man and as poor as the time he left, to find rest in the arms of Solveig, the sweetheart of his youth who had remained faithful to him all these years.

The Last Spring. This comes from the two Elegiac Melodies for String Orchestra. Originally composed as a setting for a poem called *Spring*, it has not the usual joyful atmosphere that the season implies, but rather a deep sadness, a song of lamentation as expressed in the poet's verses.

'Ich Liebe Dich' ('I Love Thee'), the best known and loveliest of Grieg's songs, is a setting of verses by Hans Christian Andersen and one of a group known as 'Melodies of the Heart'. Grieg composed it expressly for his fiancée, Nina Hagerup, whom he later married.

> *I lately saw two bright brown eyes:*
> *In them my home, my whole world lies.*

GEORG FRIDERIC HANDEL

(1685–1759)

In Poets' Corner, Westminster Abbey, in the tomb of Georg Frideric Handel his remains have lain quietly for over two hundred years. The effigy above shows him seated at a table, pen in hand, with the score of *Messiah* in front of him open at the aria 'I know that my Redeemer liveth'. This was the man whom Beethoven called 'the greatest composer who ever lived'.

Handel was born in Halle in Saxony, and from his earliest childhood he was passionately fond of music. Like so many others, however, he encountered parental opposition to any thoughts of a musical education. Up in the garret of their house, as a child of seven, and doubtless with the connivance of a servant, he had hidden a spinet whose dampened sound could not be heard below. Here, without any assistance, we are told that he taught himself to play.

On a visit with his father to the Duke of Saxe-Weissenfels one day, he was heard playing the organ after the service in the Court Chapel. Expecting a reprimand, he received instead a present from the duke who, enraptured by the boy's performance, extracted a promise from his father that young Handel would be allowed to study music. He became the pupil of the Halle organist, Zachau, who also taught him the violin. After three years Zachau told Handel with kindly pride that he already knew more than his master, and he was sent to Berlin for further study.

His father died when he was twelve and the boy was expected to earn some money. He was taken on as organist at the cathedral in Halle, during which time he composed many works for the church. But finding his life very limiting, he decided to seek his fortune in Hamburg which was then a great musical centre. Here he obtained a position as second violin in the Opera House orchestra, deputizing on occasion for the harpsichordist who, in those days, was the principal person in the orchestra, there being no conductor.

About this time Handel received an 'offer of marriage'. He

could succeed the great Buxtehude as organist at Lübeck if he married his unattractive daughter, who went with the job. In blessed single state, Handel hurriedly returned to Hamburg—this same 'generous' offer was later refused by Bach as well!

In Hamburg Handel composed his first opera, *Almira*, which was performed with great success. Three more operas followed, but they were not so readily accepted. He took his leave of Hamburg in 1706, aged twenty-one, and journeyed to Italy where he travelled widely, astounding his audiences with his skill at the harpsichord. His visit looked like developing into something of a triumphal tour. In Florence, where his fame had preceded him, he produced his first Italian opera which earned for him more than he had ever received before. Gifts were showered upon him, and he was welcomed everywhere. He took Venice by storm and filled the theatre at every performance. One night during the Carnival, a masked Handel seated himself at a harpsichord and began to play. Domenico Scarlatti, Italy's finest harpsichordist at the time, happened to enter. Catching the sound of the music he paused for a moment, as if surprised by the glorious strains he heard above the chatter. Then making his way across the room he shouted: 'It is either the Saxon or the very devil himself!' It was said that Scarlatti, whenever he was complimented on his own playing, used to pronounce Handel's name, and cross himself.

In 1709 Handel's career took a different turn. He accepted the post of Chapel Master to the Elector of Hanover, who was later to become King George I of England. Handel had scarcely settled down in his new appointment when he received news that encouraged him to go to London. He was invited to compose a special opera for the occasion of his visit, and *Rinaldo*, completed in two weeks, created a furore; Handel was the talk of the town. Reluctantly, he had to leave to resume his duties in Hanover, but within two years he had returned to settle in England permanently. He anglicized his name, and London became his home from that moment on.

It was here that he composed some of his finest masterworks and was constantly in the public eye and ear. But there were times when rival factions in the opera world tried hard to destroy him. Disappointment was frequently his lot when he refused to recognize the change in public taste. He dissipated his fortune and found himself greatly in debt. Yet he was able to overcome these tribulations, and the intensive years of activity that followed restored much of the popularity that had been his before.

We now come to a point in Handel's life when, having been in London for a quarter of a century and having composed over forty operas, he turned his hand to oratorio. 'I think, after all,' he said, 'that sacred music is best suited for a man descending in the vale of years.' With *Saul* in 1738, *Israel in Egypt* in the following year, and then *Messiah*, he was responsible for introducing the greatest period in oratorio history. *Samson, Semele, Judas Maccabaeus, Solomon, Jephtha*—a whole host of wonderful compositions came from his pen in an unceasing flow. He composed easily and untiringly.

It is interesting to look back at some of the opinions of the time, not just Handel's own, but those of his admirers and enemies too. *Theodora*, the least popular of his oratorios, was one of his great favourites. He used to say that the chorus 'He saw the Lovely Youth' was finer than anything in *Messiah*. When *Deborah* was produced, certain sections of the public reviled him in the most despicable way. He was spared no slander; he was called a swindler, a raving idiot, a false friend and a profane fellow to whom not even Holy Writ was sacred. But of the chorus in *Joshua*—'The Nations tremble', now entirely forgotten—Haydn observed that 'only one inspired author ever did or ever would pen so sublime a composition'.

Though Handel began as a composer of operas, he is best remembered by his oratorios. He also distinguished himself in his orchestral music, which is often compared with that of his contemporary, Bach. Handel's *Concerti Grossi*—the second set of twelve he composed in a little over a month—remain standard works in the repertoire of chamber orchestras. He wrote extensively for various solo instruments, and his organ concertos, of which he made a feature in the intervals of his oratorio performances, are still very popular with music lovers everywhere.

In a crowded life Handel produced such a quantity of music that the complete edition of his work, published by the German Handel Society, runs to a hundred volumes.

While composing *Jephtha* in 1751, he became partially blind, although this, his last oratorio, was nevertheless completed. A year later total darkness settled upon him and he almost ceased to compose, but not to play. He desired now to be at peace with all men, and devoted much of his time during his last years to charitable causes. When he knew that death was near, he expressed a wish that he might breathe his last on Good Friday: 'In hopes', he said, 'of meeting our Lord and Saviour on the day of his resurrection.' The actual day and hour of his passing have been the subject of some conjecture, but the inscription beneath his monument reads:

'Died on Good Friday, April XIV MDCCLIX'

Messiah. Handel composed his great masterpiece in less than twenty-five days and chose Dublin for its first performance. He had been there several months previously, at the invitation of the Lord Lieutenant, to give a series of concerts. Now all Dublin was waiting for Mr Handel's new oratorio, (The) *Messiah*, which, they said, he had composed in England specially for them. A memorable day was 13 April 1742; ladies were asked to leave their hoops at home in order to make more room. In comment, I can do no better than quote a journal of the time:

'On Tuesday last Mr Handel's sacred Grand Oratorio, The *Messiah*, was performed in the New Musick Hall in Fishamble Street: the best judges allowed it to be the most finished piece of Musick. Words are wanting to express the exquisite delight it afforded to the admiring crowded audience. The Sublime, the Grand and the Tender, adapted to the most elevated, majestick and moving Words, conspired to transport and charm the ravished Heart and Ear. It is but Justice to Mr Handel that the World should know he generously gave the Money arising from this Grand Performance to be equally shared by the Society for relieving Prisoners, the Charitable Infirmary, and Mercer's Hospital, for which they will ever gratefully remember his Name.'

Messiah was first produced in London in March 1743 at the Covent Garden Theatre. From 1750 to 1758, Handel conducted the work each year in the Chapel of the Foundling Hospital in Bloomsbury, for the benefit of that institution.

Limited space forbids me to describe in detail many of the *Messiah*'s wonderful pages, but one must mention the *Hallelujah* Chorus which stands alone. It is told that when Handel had completed this inspired burst of praise, his servant found him at his writing table staring into space as he whispered: 'I did think I did see all Heaven before me, and the Great God Himself.'

The custom of standing while this chorus is being sung dates from its first London performance. The king was so moved that he rose to his feet on impulse and the audience spontaneously followed him.

'Zadok the Priest' is one of four anthems written in 1727 for the Coronation of George II; it has remained a part of the service ever since. The quotation is from the first Book of Kings, 'Zadok the Priest and Nathan the Prophet anointed Solomon King'.

'Where'er you walk' comes from *Semele*, an opera in the style of an oratorio. Based on a libretto by Congreve, it was first produced at Covent Garden in 1744. The story is of classical origin and was described by Handel as 'a fable of no significance', though it aroused some opposition at the time. This lovely aria and 'O Sleep, Why dost thou leave me?' are the two particular reminders we have of it today.

'Silent Worship', an aria known and loved by the Victorians under this title, remains popular, and is all that we know of one of Handel's least successful operas, *Tolomeo* ('Ptolemy'). It was overshadowed and its style satirized by *The Beggar's Opera* in the same year, 1728, since when it has hardly ever been heard.

'Largo—Ombra Mai fu', the one memorable tune from Handel's only light-hearted opera, *Serse* ('Xerxes'), of 1738. Both as an aria and as an orchestral piece—not forgetting the organ versions —it is now usually regarded as a religious melody, and a solemn one at that, when it is in fact nothing more than a serenade to a tree in whose shade the singer welcomes the chance to rest awhile.

'Waft her angels' (*Jephtha*). Handel was now sixty-seven and though blindness was imminent and he well knew that this could be his last, he managed to complete *Jephtha* which is one of the finest of all his oratorios. The aria is a prayer uttered by Jephtha when he sacrifices his only daughter in observance of a sacred vow.

The *Water Music* was written for a royal party on the River Thames in the summer of 1717. King George I was in one barge while, as a newspaper of the time reported, 'a City Company's barge was employed for the music, wherein were fifty instruments of all sorts, who played all the way from Lambeth as far as Chelsea, the finest symphonies, composed expressly for this occasion by Mr Handel, which his Majesty liked so well that he caused it to be played over three times in going and returning'. Nowadays the music is mainly heard in the suite for modern orchestra, arranged by Sir Hamilton Harty from the twenty-one pieces that comprised Handel's original work.

Music for the Royal Fireworks. There were actually fireworks in 1749 in London, just about where Piccadilly is now. The festive occasion was to celebrate a peace treaty between England and France, and it was said that the music was much more exciting than the pyrotechnics, which did little more than cause a fire and start something of a stampede. Listeners today are more familiar with the music in Sir Hamilton Harty's four-movement suite.

The *Arrival of the Queen of Sheba* is a piece of music that stands high on the list of Your Hundred Best Tunes. This sparkling Sinfonia from *Solomon* is perhaps the one piece by which the oratorio is remembered. The tune was borrowed—as so frequently happened —from an earlier Italian composer. It was also arranged by Handel as a trio for wind instruments.

Berenice—Minuet. This is part of the overture, a lovely melody that has stood the test of time. It is justly famous, while the opera itself seems to have disappeared, and revivals since its first production in 1737 have been scarce indeed.

JOSEPH HAYDN

(1732–1809)

'Papa Haydn', Mozart used to call him, this generous kind-hearted soul who, looking back on his life in his later years, said: ' Almighty God, to whom I render thanks for all his unnumbered mercies, gave me such facility in music that by the time I was six, I stood up like a man and sang masses in the church choir, and could play a little on the harpsichord and violin.'

The son of the village wheelwright, Haydn was born in Rohrau, about thirty miles from Vienna on the Austrian border with Hungary. When he was eight he entered the choir school of St Stephen's Cathedral in Vienna. It was not a very happy time for him because, as he said later, 'I got more beatings than food'. At thirteen he tried his hand at writing a mass which was reputedly cruelly laughed at by his master. With hoarded money Haydn purchased two famous books of instruction and set to work to teach himself; these books were the basis of his musical education.

When his voice broke—he was sixteen—he was forced to leave the choir school, homeless and without money. Fending for himself he was able to earn a little by giving lessons, and, like most struggling musicians, he sometimes made up a serenading party to supplement his scanty income and keep alive. These serenading parties were a summer tradition in the streets of Vienna. Right through the night 'crowds would gather round the players, clapping, applauding and seldom dispersing till the serenade was over, when they would troop after the players to another district'.

A piece of good fortune came Haydn's way when he met the

famous Italian singing master, Niccola Porpora, who had the reputation of being a crusty, ill-tempered old man. Haydn wanted to learn, and no one could help him more than Porpora, so he was prepared to humble himself and carry out any menial task the master required of him. He cleaned Porpora's boots, trimmed his wig, brushed his clothes, ran his errands and was a devoted servant. Eventually he became his master's accompanist and was now able to meet many famous musicians and people influential in court circles, for Porpora knew them all.

In this way he secured an engagement as Kapellmeister to Count Morzin at his Bohemian estate. The count preferred his chief musicians to be married, so Haydn, now twenty-eight, took as his wife Maria Anna Keller, daughter of a barber who had befriended and sheltered him when he was homeless after leaving St Stephen's. Unhappily the marriage was short-lived and they separated. So was his engagement with the count who, because of financial pressures, had to disband his orchestra.

But Haydn was now quite well known, and he received an invitation to become the director of music to Prince Esterhazy, a scion of the greatest of the Hungarian noble families. This was a highly esteemed position which Haydn was to occupy for thirty years, during which time he wrote some of his finest works. Of this part of his life he said: 'I was cut off from the world, there was no one to confuse or torment me and I was forced to be original.' He lived contentedly and composed fruitfully, and the work of this thirty years spread his fame across Europe.

A few days after the death of his patron, he had a visit from a gentleman who announced himself as 'Salomon of London'. 'I have come to carry you off with me,' he said. 'We will strike a bargain tomorrow.' John Peter Salomon was an impresario, and he engaged Haydn to give twenty concerts in the year at fifty pounds each. He was to compose new symphonies and conduct them in person, seated at the piano. On 11 March 1791, at the Hanover Square Rooms, Haydn gave the first of these concerts. 'The sight of that renowned composer,' wrote Dr Burney, 'electrified the audience and awakened such a degree of enthusiasm as almost amounted to frenzy.' Everywhere Haydn's reception delighted him. He met the great of the land, and was applauded wherever he appeared.

Upon his return to Vienna he settled in a little cottage just outside the city. There were still great works to come, including *The*

Creation and *The Seasons*, the success of which was immediate and formed the crowning achievements of his latter years.

The number of his compositions is estimated to be in the region of eight hundred, of which the hundred and four (catalogued) symphonies and the eighty-four string quartets are the mainstay of an output that stamped Haydn as one of the greatest composers ever.

The Creation. During the whole of his life, Haydn held a simple and touching religious faith. It was his custom to head his work 'In nomine Domini' ('In the name of the Lord'), and end it with 'Laus Deo' ('Praise be to God'). Now, at the age of sixty-four, he wished to fulfil an ambition to emulate Handel whom he had long admired by writing an oratorio. With a text based on the Book of Genesis and Milton's poem *Paradise Lost*, he was deeply conscious that he was embarking on a great work and set about his task in the spirit of the deepest humility. 'I was never so devout as when I was at work on *The Creation*,' he said. 'I fell on my knees each day and begged God to give me strength to accomplish the work successfully.'

The oratorio was completed after a year and a half of intensive and exhausting labour. It had its first performance in April 1798 at which Haydn himself conducted and was so emotionally affected that he feared he would have a stroke. 'One moment I was cold as ice, the next I was on fire,' he said.

The Creation met with instantaneous success, and within a short time all Europe was resounding to its magnificent music. Of its many favoured numbers, the most requested is undoubtedly the mighty chorus that concludes the first part, 'The Heavens are telling'.

Symphony no. 45 in F Sharp Minor, the *Farewell* Symphony. The most famous of Haydn's earlier symphonies, this was composed in 1772, and was intended as a respectful hint to Prince Esterhazy that the members of his orchestra needed a holiday. As the final movement neared its end, the musicians, one by one, snuffed the candles on their music stands and tiptoed out. The last notes were played by two remaining violinists, who then did likewise, and left the stage to silence and to darkness. The prince, we are told, was most amused and readily took the hint.

Symphony no. 94 in G, the *Surprise* Symphony. Belonging to the Salomon period, this is the best known of all Haydn's symphonies. Its nickname stems from the 'little joke' in the second movement, an *andante* based on a Croatian folk air. The movement opens gently with a quiet statement of the theme. Then suddenly come the startling, crashing chords from the full orchestra. Haydn denied that he included this effect to make the ladies scream, or to awaken the audience and make them sit up and listen in case they were nodding!

Symphony no. 101 in D, the *Clock* Symphony. The eleventh in the Salomon series, this gets its name from the constant tick-tock rhythm in the second movement. Though altogether an attractive symphony, it would appear that this clock-like effect more than anything else has attracted itself to listeners.

Serenade from the String Quartet opus 3 no. 5. In recent years the second movement of this quartet in F has become extremely popular in arrangements for string orchestra. Sometimes known simply as '*Serenade* by Haydn', it has achieved a fame of its own. Though attributed to Haydn, it has been suggested that it could have been composed by an obscure contemporary of his named Hofstetter.

GUSTAV HOLST

(1874–1934)

Throughout his life Holst was a somewhat puzzling figure, both as a man and as a musician. It was said that he lacked human warmth and had little taste for social niceties. Though shy and retiring he was not lonely, for it was he who chose solitude the better to surrender himself entirely to his work.

He was born in Cheltenham, and suffered ill health from his earliest childhood. As a young man he followed the path of an ascetic, and when he was a student at the Royal College of Music he was regarded as rather eccentric. He studied the trombone, and it was not unusual to see him, with his instrument slung on his back, walking home to Cheltenham.

By the time he was twenty his first compositions were being performed and he was beginning to cultivate a style of his own. He introduced folksong elements into his music, and among his most delightful works are his choral arrangements of traditional airs. He was a prolific composer who was uncompromising in his integrity; he looked neither for fame nor the plaudits of the crowd. From 1905 until the end of his life he was director of music at St Paul's Girls' School in London. These were his happiest years. In his sound-proof study here he composed his finest works.

While little of what he wrote can be called popular, one work particularly is known to all who listen to music.

The Planets dates from 1916 and is Holst's most important orchestral work. It is a Suite consisting of seven sections: Mars—The Bringer of War; Venus—The Bringer of Peace; Mercury—The Winged Messenger; Jupiter—The Bringer of Jollity; Saturn—The Bringer of Old Age; Uranus—The Magician; and Neptune—The Mystic.

Holst himself gave us a clue to the nature of the music when he explained that these pieces were suggested by the astrological significance of the stars, and had no connection with the gods of classical mythology. Each of the sections creates its own mood, and although there is no link between them, the contrasting effect of each with its neighbour makes the whole a work of outstanding brilliance.

'The Holy City'

'The Holy City', one of our best-loved sacred songs, was composed in 1892 by Stephen Adams, the *nom de plume* of Michael Maybrick (1844–1913), a well-known baritone of his day. He and Frederick E. Weatherly (1848–1929), who together wrote the words of this and a number of other popular ballads such as 'Nirvana' and 'Thora', were a most successful song-writing partnership. Weatherly was a barrister who was made a King's Counsel in 1925. His lyrics include 'Danny Boy', 'Roses of Picardy' and 'The Star of Bethlehem', and he produced the first English versions of Mascagni's opera *Cavalleria Rusticana* and Leoncavallo's *I Pagliacci*.

'In a Monastery Garden'

Composed in 1912 by Albert Ketelby (the pen-name of William Aston (1875–1959)) a composer of light music that was extremely popular with a wide audience between the wars. With such pieces as 'In a Persian Market', 'Bells across the Meadow' and 'The Sanctuary of the Heart', though perhaps less frequently heard today, 'In a Monastery Garden' is still remembered with affection by listeners of an earlier generation. Ketelby also conducted orchestras at several London theatres.

FRANZ LEHÁR
(1870–1948)

Franz Lehár's father was a regimental bandmaster who was garri-risoned at Komorn in Hungary when his son was born. There was no doubt in his mind that the boy would be a musician, and before Franz could even read or write he was taught the violin and piano, and when he was twelve he applied to the Prague Academy and passed the entrance examination with flying colours.

During his six years there he came to the notice of Dvořák who showed much interest in his compositions. Dvořák's advice to him was, 'Hang up your fiddle and write music'; but his father was not so sure. 'A good violinist is never lost,' he told his son; 'he can always make a living.' A year after leaving the Academy Franz found himself first violin in his father's band—he was now a corporal in the 87th Imperial and Royal Infantry Regiment.

By the time he was twenty-six he had had an opera produced, word of which had reached Gustav Mahler, who seriously con-sidered presenting it at the Vienna Opera. Vienna for young Lehár was the magical city, the hub of the world's music and also where his heart was. So to Vienna he went as a bandmaster. His first success came in 1902 with an operetta called *Viennese Women*. Now out of uniform, he devoted himself entirely to composition which, in the course of the next few years, was to establish him as the rightful heir to the throne of Johann Strauss, as the King of Viennese melody.

Although Lehár wrote twenty-three operettas (not counting revised versions) there is only room here to talk about *The Merry Widow*, the greatest of them all.

***

The Merry Widow. Although this made Lehár world famous, he had not been the first choice for its composer. This honour had gone to Richard Heuberger, whose masterpiece, *The Opera Ball*, was then all the rage. But Heuberger's first attempts at *The Merry Widow* were so unsatisfactory that he himself gave up the commission. *The Merry Widow* was in fact in the nature of a stop-gap. The Theater-an-der-Wien had just produced a failure and was empty, so rehearsals of Lehár's operetta were hurried on. It opened on 30 December 1905 and, contrary to belief, was not a 'smash hit' at its first performance. One critic went so far as to say that he 'considered it the most distasteful he had ever seen'. In the early weeks of its run it was poorly attended, then quite suddenly it took hold and all Vienna began to talk about it.

It came to London in 1907, and at Daly's Theatre with Lily Elsie in the title role it ran for nearly eight hundred performances. Its success was so far-reaching that at one time, in Buenos Aires, it played in five different theatres in five different languages. The passing years have not diminished the freshness of its music. 'Vilja' and its famous waltz are among the many *Merry Widow* tunes that never fail to delight us still.

FRANZ LISZT

(1811–1886)

Liszt himself perhaps best described his own complex and extraordinary personality in the words: 'half gipsy, half Franciscan'. And even if we accept the portraits of him by others as 'half saint, half charlatan' and 'a mixture of priest and circus rider', we would still lack sufficient information for a full understanding of his many-sided character.

Liszt came from a small town in Hungary. At nine he demonstrated his precocious talent by playing Hummel's Piano Concerto in E Flat at a public concert. Through the generosity of Prince Esterhazy and some of his friends, a fund was raised to provide for Liszt's further musical training, and the family moved to Vienna where Franz was sent to Czerny to learn the piano, and to Salieri, Beethoven's last teacher, for composition. After no more than perhaps a dozen lessons, Czerny was so delighted with the boy's progress that he was pleased to forgo his fees.

In 1823, when he was twelve, Liszt was already a well-known figure in Vienna musical life. It is said that Beethoven was so moved by Liszt's playing at one of his concerts that he went on to the platform, lifted the boy in his arms and fondly embraced him.

Four years later Liszt's father died. His last words to his son were, 'You have a good brain and a kind heart, beware of women or they will ruin you', an admonition that seems to have been of no avail, for it is reliably recorded that Liszt in the course of his life had no fewer than twenty-six 'serious' love affairs.

His father's warning had hardly left his dying lips when Franz fell madly in love with one of his pupils, a beautiful girl of sixteen. When eventually they had to part because of her father's opposition, Liszt became so ill that there was a rumour in Paris that he was dead. He sought refuge in religion, and seriously thought of entering the priesthood. 'I hoped,' he said, 'that it might be granted me to live the life of the saints, and perhaps die the death of the martyrs.' Such was the paradox of Liszt's personality that one side of him was given to religious contemplation, while the other craved the company of women, the adulation of his audiences and a life of luxury. Indeed, in later life, he took holy orders and was granted the title of Abbé.

For almost ten years, from 1840, Liszt, in his concert tours, proved beyond doubt that he was the finest pianist of his time. He spent the last years of his life in Bayreuth, and was largely instrumental in bringing the operas of Richard Wagner to world attention. But when Wagner persuaded Liszt's daughter, Cosima, to leave her husband and live with him, Liszt was so angered that he became Wagner's implacable enemy, a breach that was later healed when they met at the first Bayreuth festival. In 1886 Liszt became seriously ill, and against his doctor's advice attended a performance of *Tristan and Isolde*. He died shortly afterwards and the last word he spoke was 'Tristan'.

❦

Piano Concerto no. 1 in E Flat is a brilliant showpiece, caustically named the 'triangle concerto' because Liszt had introduced this humble instrument into the score. For this reason it was despised by the musical snobs of the day and neglected.

It was first performed in Weimar in 1855 with Berlioz as the conductor and Liszt as the soloist, the only work by another composer during a week devoted to the music of Berlioz.

Hungarian Rhapsody no. 2. Liszt edited ten volumes of Hungarian national melodies, many of which folk tunes he incorporated in the fifteen *Hungarian Rhapsodies* he composed for the piano. Although he considered them best suited to this instrument, he did arrange some for orchestra of which no. 2 is the most famous. It has sustained a popularity beyond that accorded to any other of his works.

Liebestraum no. 3 in A Flat. This *Liebestraum* ('Love's Dream') is by far the best known of the set of three such pieces written by Liszt (we may believe) for one of his beloved ladies. They were transcribed from three of his own romantic love songs and he called them nocturnes.

Consolation no. 3. There are six *Consolations* in all inspired by a volume of French poems of the same name. Here again one alone has taken hold of the public fancy and remains the favourite of the group. It was once said of this *Consolation* that 'peace and serenity speak out of every note'.

'The Lord's Prayer'

'The Lord's Prayer'. Albert Hay Malotte, an American organist and composer, wrote this enormously successful setting of 'The Lord's Prayer' in 1935. He studied music in Paris and for a period played the organ at a London church. He spent a number of years in Hollywood writing film music, among which were the scores of some of Walt Disney's *Silly Symphonies*.

PIETRO MASCAGNI
(1863–1945)

Mascagni's life was a continual struggle against hardship. He came of simple folk, his father being a baker in Leghorn (Livorno) in Italy. Through financial help from an uncle he was able to go to Milan, where he studied under Ponchielli and was for several years the conductor of a small touring opera company. By this time he had already composed two operas that had yielded him little.

In 1888, in the middle of writing something new, he learned of a competition for a one-act opera organized by an Italian publisher. He hastened the completion of his work and sent it off. This was *Cavalleria Rusticana*, which won for him the prize and a production in Rome.

Its first performance aroused the audience to unheard-of enthusiasm. Mascagni took twenty curtain calls, and the critics hailed him as Verdi's successor. He was famous overnight. On his return to his native city he was welcomed with a torchlight procession; even the king honoured him, and at twenty-seven he was a national idol.

Though almost a dozen operas followed, including *L'Amico Fritz* and *Iris*, Mascagni's fame rests solely on *Cavalleria Rusticana*. This story of 'Rustic Chivalry' (a translation of its title) comes from a play in which the great Italian actress Duse had made a success. It was the first of the 'verismo' (true to life) operas; a hot-blooded melodrama through which runs the most impassioned music. It is set in a village square in Sicily on Easter morning.

From *Cavalleria Rusticana* comes the *Easter* hymn. While the villagers quietly wend their way to Mass, some remain outside the church to pray. Kneeling in prayer, and led by the voice of

Santuzza, the proud and defiant peasant girl who is the central figure in the story, they sing the *Resurrection* hymn, 'Let us sing of the Lord now victorious'.

The *Intermezzo*, which divides the work into two parts, is quietly played by the orchestra to an empty stage after one of the opera's most dramatic scenes. Its music foreshadows the impending tragedy.

JULES MASSENET
(1842–1912)

The music of Massenet has been variously described as graceful, suave, elegant and flowing, a reaction no doubt, if it's true, to the sounds that surrounded him as a boy. His father was an ironmaster, and young Massenet heard so much noise that he hated it. 'The clash of steel and iron and hammers vibrated throughout my childhood,' he said.

He was six when his mother gave him his first piano lesson, and he remembered well the day he started. It was 24 February 1848. He wrote later that 'the lesson was strangely interrupted by the noise of firing in the streets. The revolution had begun'.

When he went to the Conservatoire his first teacher thought him an ungifted pupil and told him: 'Don't waste your time with composition—go home and do something else.' 'I wept,' said Massenet. 'I packed my belongings and did as he suggested. I went home discouraged and broken-hearted.' But he didn't give up his music. He studied as best he could and five years later re-entered the Conservatoire, only to confound his former teacher by winning the Prix de Rome with a cantata.

Of ambition Massenet had an abundance, but of confidence, little. Strange for a man who was to become the foremost French composer of his time. He recalls that he sent one of his first scores to Pasdeloup, an eminent conductor who ran popular concerts in Paris. A week later he received a note to come and hear a rehearsal of his work, but he was too shy and afraid to go.

Massenet reached the height of his fame in 1884 with *Manon*, which ranks among the greatest successes in the history of French opera. From that time one triumph followed another, and he left in all some twenty-seven operas and a number of splendid orchestral suites.

Thaïs (*Méditation*). Based on a novel by Anatole France, the opera was first presented in Paris in 1894. It tells a story of sacred and profane love, set in Egypt in the early Christian era. As a writer on Massenet explained, it concerns 'a sinner who became a saint, and a saint who became a sinner, a courtesan who turned from the God of Love to the Love of God'. The opera's name stays before the public by reason of the *Méditation*, a hauntingly beautiful violin solo whose theme is repeated throughout.

Elégie comes from an orchestral suite made from the incidental music to a play called *Les Érynnies* ('The Furies'). Originally known as *Invocation*, it gained tremendous popularity under its present title, both as a 'cello solo and as a song of lamentation.

The *Last Sleep of the Virgin* was unheard of in this country for many years until Sir Thomas Beecham revived it and made it one of his 'lollipops'. This touchingly effective orchestral interlude is the only surviving excerpt of the oratorio *La Vierge* ('The Virgin'), which enjoyed a period of glory after it was first introduced in 1880.

FELIX MENDELSSOHN-BARTHOLDY

(1809–1847)

Most of the great composers endured hardship and often despair in their formative years, and had to overcome stern trials in acquiring the mastery of their art. In contrast, Mendelssohn's boyhood was happy in all respects, and his background distinguished. His grandfather, Moses Mendelssohn, was one of the leading philosophers of his time, his father was well to do, and the enlightened and educated atmosphere of his home served as an inspiration.

In appearance he was described as 'a beautiful youth with auburn hair clustering in ringlets round his shoulders'. The novelist Thackeray, who met him in later years, said: 'His face is the most beautiful I ever saw. Like what I imagine our Saviour's to have been.'

Mendelssohn was born in Hamburg of Jewish parents who adopted the name of Bartholdy when they embraced the Lutheran faith. It was evident from the first that he was a musical prodigy. By the time he was twelve years old he had written a couple of operas and numerous other compositions.

His parents, who had settled in Berlin when he was three, kept 'open house', a favourite meeting-place for people of distinction in the arts. Musical evenings were held regularly, and Felix was given every opportunity to perform before the guests. On these occasions there was invariably a small orchestra, and the young composer conducted his early symphonies and other of his instrumental works at them. The flow of writing continued meanwhile. He had now completed his thirteenth symphony, of which he later remarked: 'I wrote twelve symphonies before I dared to inscribe the thirteenth as number one.' Shortly afterwards his teacher told him: 'You are no longer an apprentice, but an independent member of the brotherhood of musicians. I proclaim you an independent in the name of Mozart, Haydn and the older Bach.' All this he had achieved by the time he was seventeen, in between his formal studies at Berlin University.

In 1829 he considered that the time had come for him to try his fortunes abroad. He travelled extensively, and on the first of his nine visits to England he appeared with equal success both as conductor and pianist. London was very much to his liking, and his audiences were no less pleased with him. From London he went to Scotland, whose sights and sounds were ultimately to find expression in the *Scottish* Symphony and the *Hebrides* Overture. This was the beginning of a long and close association with this country where, as a foreign composer, he stood high with Handel in the esteem of the English people.

So far I have dealt mainly with the first half of Mendelssohn's life. The major points in his career that followed included his appointment as director of the Gewandhaus Orchestra in Leipzig where he established himself as one of Europe's leading conductors. Finally he fulfilled a dream he had long nurtured, to found a conservatory of music in that city, an institution that was to produce some of the greatest musicians of future generations.

In his remaining years he worked extremely hard, giving much time to teaching at the conservatory, while continuing his concert tours both at home and abroad. His health broke down in 1847, and although weak, he insisted on going to London to direct his oratorio *Elijah*. On his return, now completely exhausted, he heard that his sister Fanny, whom he idolized, had just died, a shock which doubtless hastened his own death within three months.

Symphony no. 4 in A Major (*Italian*). The inspiration for this symphony came to Mendelssohn in the course of his travels through Italy in 1830. It was completed in Berlin two years later, and when the Philharmonic Society of London asked him to produce a symphony, overture, and a vocal piece for their 1833 season, he sent them the *Italian*, going to London himself to conduct it. The first movement, exuberant and joyous, conveys how he felt when he wrote to his sister: 'Italy at last. What I have been looking forward to all my life as the greatest happiness is now begun. I feel as if I were a young prince making his entry....'

Concerto for Violin and Orchestra in E Minor. It was the celebrated violinist, Ferdinand David (who had been Mendelssohn's concertmaster at the Gewandhaus) who urged the composition of this concerto. Mendelssohn's response was '... I have the liveliest desire to write one for you, and if I have a few propitious days, I shall bring you something of the sort ...'.

Those few days stretched into five years. David, as expected, was the soloist, and the Danish composer, Niels Gade, conducted it when it appeared to public acclaim in 1845. The concerto, which has been described as bearing '... the charm of eternal youth', has few rivals in the violin repertoire.

A Midsummer Night's Dream. Mendelssohn and his sister Fanny had been reading Shakespeare's comedy together. He was barely seventeen at the time, and was so fascinated by its fairy-tale world that he could not resist the beckoning need to put his thoughts into music. He spent the best part of a year extemporizing it on the piano, producing first a piano duet which he orchestrated as an overture and, in two months, had performed in the garden house of the Mendelssohn home. In 1827 it was introduced at a public concert and, thirteen years later, at Covent Garden, where it was played as the introduction to Shakespeare's play for the first time.

In 1843 King Frederick William IV of Prussia asked Mendelssohn to compose the incidental music for a production of *A Midsummer Night's Dream* at a new theatre in Potsdam. Mendelssohn added twelve numbers to the overture. Today, as a rule, only five of them are heard in concert programmes.

The best known is the Overture which, from the moment of its opening measures, evokes the fanciful character of Shakespeare's play, and gracefully proceeds to depict throughout its changing scenes and moods.

The Scherzo, the prelude to the second act, is perhaps the most enchanting piece of fairy music ever written, a sound-picture world of scurrying elves and goblins.

The *Wedding March.* As with all good fairy tales, this one has a happy ending. The *Wedding March* delightfully complements the bliss of all concerned in the famous tune that has become the customary 'going out' music at weddings.

The *Hebrides* Overture (*Fingal's Cave*). This seascape in music, often regarded as the perfect symphonic poem, was the result of Mendelssohn's visit to the Hebrides in 1829. At Fingal's Cave on the little island of Staffa, the bleak beauty and the surging sea dashing against the rocks so impressed him that he wrote: 'You may understand how extraordinarily the Hebrides affected me. The following came into my mind.' And here he had jotted down the first ten bars from which the whole work grew.

But its progress never quite pleased him. He told his sister: 'The middle portion smells more of counterpoint than of seagulls and salt fish.' It was nearly three years before the overture was ready, and it received its first performance at the hands of the Philharmonic Society of London in 1832, with instantaneous success.

Elijah. It is generally held that, next to *Messiah*, *Elijah* is the most popular oratorio with the British people. Mendelssohn had already found success here with his earlier biblical work, *St Paul*, and now, in 1846 at the behest of the Birmingham Festival for whom it was written, he came to direct the first performance of *Elijah*. After the première he wrote home: 'No work of mine ever went so admirably at the first performance, or was received with such enthusiasm as this.'

The whole magnificent work is brimful of marvellous passages that include the immortal tenor aria, 'If with all your hearts', Elijah's strong calm prayer, 'Lord God of Abraham', and one of the most beautiful soprano songs ever written, 'Hear Ye Israel', which is followed by the whole power of orchestra, chorus and organ in the mighty 'Be Not Afraid'. And finally, 'O Rest in the Lord', the richness of whose tender melody entrances the listener and brings back to the memory of all who have heard it the famous recording by Kathleen Ferrier.

'O for the Wings of a Dove', from the hymn 'Hear My Prayer' which was composed in 1844 for soprano accompanied by choir and organ. This ranks among the best of Mendelssohn's short sacred pieces and, beloved of the Victorians, it finds no less favour with choral groups and church choirs today. It was one of three works submitted at the request of William Bartholomew of London, a musician and a man of many talents, who had translated and adapted a number of the texts of Mendelssohn's compositions. Bartholomew chose 'Hear My Prayer', a paraphrase of some verses from Psalm 55 whose second section 'O For the Wings of a Dove' is perhaps the more familiar part of the hymn. It is particularly popular as a vehicle for boy singers.

WOLFGANG AMADEUS MOZART

(1756–1791)

'I tell you before God, and as an honest man, that your son is the greatest composer I know, either personally or by name.' So said Haydn to Mozart's father, Leopold.

Leopold, himself a well-known musician in Salzburg, was quick to recognize his son's remarkable gifts. Perhaps it would be unfair to say that he was too ready to exploit him, but at the age of six nevertheless, Wolfgang, with his highly talented sister Maria Anna, was taken by their father on a grand tour and 'exhibited' in the leading concert halls and before the royalty and nobility of Europe. In Frankfurt, for instance, a newspaper reported that 'the boy, who is in his seventh year, will play a Concerto for the Violin, and will accompany symphonies on the clavier, the keyboard being covered with a cloth, and he will play with as much facility as if he could see the keys. He will instantly name the notes played, whether singly or in chords, on the clavier or any other instrument, bell, glass, or clock. He will finally, both on the harpsichord and the organ, improvise for as long as may be desired, and in any key. . . .'

These 'show business' stunts were to continue for a number of years. It is true that the musicians of Europe stood aghast, and there were such comments as 'he is so extraordinary a phenomenon that one finds it difficult to believe unless one has seen him with one's own eyes and heard him with one's own ears'.

Of their visit to London in 1764 Leopold wrote: 'On May 19 we were brought to court, and were from six to ten o'clock with the King and Queen. The King first put before Wolfgang pieces by Bach (Christian), Abel and Handel. He played them all at sight. . . . He accompanied the Queen in a song. . . . He took the bass of a Handel aria and improvised a most beautiful melody on it to the astonishment of all.'

The Mozarts were on their travels for almost four years. When they returned home Wolfgang came under the patronage of the Archbishop of Salzburg, who made him a concertmaster. Leopold, however, wished his son to continue his studies and his concerts abroad. But by this time the infant prodigy was no longer an infant, and his sensational feats were beginning to lose their appeal for a blasé public. Hitherto he had been welcomed as a child rather than for his music, miraculous though his performances were. At each concert he played his own latest compositions, symphonies, concertos, music of all kinds (as a composer he was far from idle). He could write anywhere and under any conditions, and he made such progress that by the time he was sixteen at least a hundred and fifty works, including two operas, bore his name.

The four years following his return to Salzburg (from the ages of seventeen to twenty-one) proved a most unhappy period for him. He complained that 'I live in a country where music meets with little success'. The archbishop who had befriended him had died, and his successor treated Mozart with scant respect; his work was unappreciated and his pay was poor. Most of the other musicians at the archbishop's court were a disreputable band who were more concerned with spending their time in the inns round about. Mozart had little or nothing in common with them and found it hard to live in such company. He felt he had to escape and so, much against his will, the archbishop granted him leave.

Mozart was away for over a year, and though he averred that his journey had not been useless he made little money and there was still no sign of the security he sought. His dislike of Salzburg grew more intense than ever, although within two years as a result of his last tour, he received a commission to compose an opera for the Munich Carnival of 1781.

The opera *Idomeneo*, his most ambitious work so far, gave him his first real taste of success which led him to believe that his good fortune was now beginning. His decision to leave Salzburg was hastened by a stormy episode with the archbishop, who 'blazed like a fire' and called Mozart a scoundrel, a knave and a scurvy fellow. Now in open revolt, Mozart submitted his resignation, and for his pains was summarily thrown out by one of the archbishop's stewards. Thus he took leave of his native city for good and went to settle in Vienna. In the following year, 1782, Mozart married Constanze Weber, and they had six children of whom only two survived beyond the first year of their birth.

Though Mozart's prestige was growing rapidly and he was writing some of his most important works—culminating in 1786 with *The Marriage of Figaro*—he was constantly experiencing periods of utter dejection. His work was miserably rewarded and his financial position precarious. There were long intervals when he earned very little, and he was frequently forced to call on publishers and friends for loans to tide him over.

In the last years of his life, although at the zenith of his fame and popularity, he was in a state of destitution, and his wife was an invalid for whom he had to procure every necessary comfort. Notwithstanding these ill-conditioned times he continued to compose one glorious work after another, and *Don Giovanni*, for instance, was greeted with greater enthusiasm than any of his other, previous works. During the next few months following this he produced his last three magnificent symphonies.

In 1791 he entered upon his thirty-sixth and last year. Into it he crowded, among much other music, the Clarinet Concerto and *The Magic Flute*. All Vienna rang with praise for this last opera while his life was ebbing to its close. Too late he was offered appointments and commissions for which he had longed all his life. His remaining days were spent feverishly writing the *Requiem*. On the evening of 5 December, his wife and his friend and pupil Süssmayer were with him. The score of the *Requiem* lay open on the bed, while Mozart tried feebly to communicate to Süssmayer certain details as to its completion. Towards midnight he turned his face to the wall as if to sleep, and within the hour he had breathed his last. In the words of one of his many biographers, 'the world had waited eight centuries for him, and he was to remain only for a moment'.

Constanze was so overcome with grief that she was too distraught to attend his funeral the next day. On a wild and stormy December morning a service was held at St Stephen's Church with a mere five of his friends in attendance. As the body was carried through the deserted streets, the weather became so bad that the party was forced to turn back, so that no single friend or acquaintance was there when Mozart's coffin, together with some fifteen others, was interred in the common burial ground of the poor. When Constanze was better she visited the cemetery, but no one could tell her the exact location of the grave, and to this day no stone remains to mark the spot where the body of Wolfgang Amadeus Mozart lies.

In the following brief comments on the selected Mozart pieces, you will note after some the letter 'K' followed by a number. This stands for (Ludwig) Köchel, who in 1862 compiled the first standard catalogue of Mozart's works, thereby giving them all a 'Köchel' listing.

Symphony no. 39 in E Flat Major (K. 543). Mozart's three last and greatest symphonies were all composed within seven weeks in the summer of 1788, and represent the crowning achievement of his orchestral music.

This, the first of them, was written at a time when his baby daughter was dying, and he was in a mood of deepest despair. That he was able under these circumstances to produce such 'a joyous utterance' is more than sufficient testimony of his genius. It is a consistently delightful work of which the third movement is one of his most beautiful minuets.

Symphony no. 40 in G Minor (K. 550). This has probably evoked as much ecstatic praise as any piece of music ever written, including such tributes as, 'There are few things in art that are perfect. The G Minor Symphony is one of them.' Schubert said he could hear the angels singing through the music. The symphony flows with a succession of lovely themes with, here and there, a tinge of melancholy. It has an *andante* of sublime beauty and a lively minuet.

Symphony no. 41 in C Major (*Jupiter*) (K. 551). This, the last of the three great symphonies of the summer of 1788, was written in fifteen days.

The *Jupiter* title was supposedly given by the music publisher

J. B. Cramer because of the symphony's 'loftiness of ideas and nobility of treatment'. The name was apparently mentioned first in the programme of a Philharmonic Society concert in London in 1821.

Scholars, critics and musicians all agree that Mozart reached his highest art in this symphony, and some regard the *andante cantabile* as perhaps the finest of all his slow movements.

Piano Concerto no. 20 in D Minor (K. 466). Mozart himself was the soloist at the first performance of this concerto in Vienna in 1785. According to his father, the orchestral parts were hardly ready in time, and Mozart was at the copyists' up to the last moment before hurrying off to the concert. It was played without a rehearsal, but Leopold tells us 'it was magnificent'.

Piano Concerto no. 23 in A Major (K. 488). This was one of three piano concertos that Mozart composed in quick succession in 1786. No doubt, in his usual financial straits, he wanted to present them at the Lenten Concerts, Lent being a particularly lucrative season in the Vienna of those days.

Again, Mozart was the soloist in a performance that called forth this memory from one who was present: 'I cannot describe my astonishment when I happened to be so fortunate as to hear the immortal W. A. Mozart. . . . I had never been accustomed to hear anything so great or so wonderful. . . . Even to this day, although a very old man, I can still hear those heavenly harmonies, and die in the firm conviction that there has only been one Mozart.'

Horn Concerto no. 4 in E Flat (K. 495). The rondo of this concerto is perhaps the best-known piece of all Mozart's horn music—or so it is for my listeners at least, who have made it one of their 'best tunes'.

The concerto was originally written for a prominent horn

player, Ignaz Leutgeb, who kept a cheese shop in his spare time. So outstanding a performer was he that most of the horn music of the period was written with him in mind.

Eine Kleine Nachtmusik. 'A little night music' is the translation of its German title, but this music is more than just 'little'. It is an elegant serenade for strings only, that clearly suggests music out of doors and under the stars. The beautiful melodies woven into its four movements (each movement is a gem) blend with the others to form an exceptional work that is probably the most widely played of all Mozart's orchestral compositions.

Ave Verum Corpus. In the summer of 1791 Constanze was expecting another child and went to Baden for her health. While Mozart was visiting her he composed this motet, the first piece of church music he had written for eight years. These few bars of heavenly music are of the utmost simplicity and stand as one of his memorable inspirations.

Laudate Dominum (K. 339). This is the penultimate section of the *Vesperae Solennes de Confessore,* the second of two Vesper Services that Mozart wrote in 1780 as part of his duties as principal composer at the archbishop's court in Salzburg. The *Laudate Dominum,* a setting of Psalm 117 for four voices, orchestra and organ, has remained popular with listeners everywhere.

The Marriage of Figaro is an opera based on the French comedy by Beaumarchais, whose sequel was the model that Rossini used later for *The Barber of Seville.* The libretto was thought at first to smack too much of political satire, so that the emperor forbade its performance until he was assured of the removal of 'all that might give offence'. It had its first performance in Vienna in 1786. Michael Kelly, the Irish tenor who took part in it, wrote in his memoirs: 'The theatre was packed, and so many arias were repeated that the length of the opera was very nearly doubled. . . . I thought the orchestra would never cease applauding, beating their violin bows against the music stands. . . . The emperor himself cried loudly "Bravo!".'

For all that, the opera was withdrawn after nine performances and it was several years before it received its due recognition. In a score rich in lovely melodies, the scintillating Overture is a perfect prelude. 'Non piu andrai', Figaro's lively song, is the first act finale. The opera's best-known number is perhaps the soprano aria, 'Voi che sapete', and one of the most beautiful of all Mozart's arias is 'Dove Sono'.

Don Giovanni. There have been many operas based on the subject of Don Juan, but none has enjoyed quite the popularity of this version by Mozart. It was commissioned by the Prague Opera and first presented there in 1787. It is said that the Overture was composed in three hours, on the night before the opening performance.

According to a newspaper of the time, connoisseurs were agreed that such a performance had never before been witnessed in Prague. Mozart himself was the conductor, and his appearance in the orchestra was the signal for cheers which were renewed at his exit. The numbers we know best are the *Catalogue* Song, 'Madamina', in which Leporello, Don Giovanni's servant, runs through the list of his master's conquests; 'La Ci darem la mano' ('There we will hold hands'), a duet of great beauty; and one of the most famous tenor arias in all opera, 'Il Mio tesoro' ('Speak for me to my lady').

'My Love is like a Red, Red Rose'

The words of this song are by Robert Burns, but the air—called 'Low down in the broom'—had been set in varied form and to several lyrics previously. The origin of the melody is obscure but is believed to derive from a Scottish folksong of the sixteen hundreds. 'Low down in the broom' was also known in Sussex as late as this century. Beethoven used a variant of the tune for 'Ye shepherds of this pleasant vale' in his set of Scottish folksong arrangements.

JACQUES OFFENBACH

(1819–1880)

Rossini, who had something to say about most of the composers he knew, called Offenbach 'the Mozart of the Champs Élysées'. For over two decades Offenbach was perhaps the most outstanding composer of light opera in Europe. During this time he wrote about a hundred works for the stage.

He was born in Cologne, in Germany, the son of a synagogue cantor. At fourteen Jacques was already an excellent 'cellist, but his application for a place at the Paris Conservatoire was turned down because their rules denied admission to anyone of foreign birth. His father, however, prevailed upon the then director, Cherubini, who, when he heard the boy play, agreed to relax the rules and accept him.

After his time at the Conservatoire, Offenbach played in the orchestra of the Opéra-Comique, a job which he tolerated lightheartedly. His fines for 'misbehaviour' more often than not considerably reduced his salary.

But his thoughts were only for a career as a composer. His idea was to have a theatre of his own which would be a place for music of wit and gaiety. Before the opportunity presented itself he spent five years as the musical director of the Comédie Française. When a small run-down theatre did become available, he saw his chance. He renamed it the 'Bouffes Parisiens', and six weeks later opened with a mixed bill which included a pantomime and a musical farce composed by himself. The entertainment was a sensation and became the talk of Paris. This was the beginning that led ultimately to his production of *Orpheus in the Underworld*, the success of which was to make Offenbach a world figure.

Towards the end of his life his one wish was to complete the opera on which he had been working for some years, and which he hoped would be his highest achievement. This was *The Tales of Hoffman*, which he would not live to see performed. He died revered, but with his passing came the end of an era.

Orpheus in the Underworld. In its early days not everyone was prepared to accept this parody of the classical legend of the Olympian Gods. It was seen by some as a blasphemy on 'holy and glorious antiquity', and was called 'brothel music' by others. No matter, because the public at large has always enjoyed every minute of it. Offenbach's score sparkles with the brightest of comic music, including the Overture, the famous *Can Can*, and the breezy song 'If I were King of the Beotians', as particular favourites. The latter is especially popular with British listeners in the version made by Geoffrey Dunn for Sadler's Wells.

The Tales of Hoffman. Based on some episodes from the fantastic tales by the German author E. T. A. Hoffman, this opera was first produced in Paris four months after Offenbach died in 1880.

Exquisitely tender pages are interspersed with the most colourful of music, as varied as the incidents themselves. Its melodic delights include, of course, the famous *Barcarolle*, one of the best-loved tunes in the realm of opera.

SIR HUBERT PARRY
(1848–1918)

Though much of his music has fallen into neglect Sir Hubert Parry was one of the most eminent English composers of the last two hundred years. He wrote prolifically in a variety of forms, and his output included five symphonies.

His first work to reach the public was an Intermezzo for Strings in 1868 at the Gloucester Festival where, for a number of years, his works received regular performances. There is a tablet to his memory in Gloucester Cathedral. With the production of *Blest Pair of Sirens*, a setting of Milton's ode, he was recognized as an accomplished and inspired composer.

In 1894 he was appointed director of the Royal College of Music, a post he retained for the rest of his life. Some regard his choral work *Job* as his finest achievement, but to the public at large 'Jerusalem' is perhaps the only composition by which he is widely remembered. One of the many unison songs that Parry wrote for children, it was composed in 1916 to words from William Blake's poem *Milton* and immediately became a great popular success. It remains to this day one of our great national songs. For the Leeds Festival of 1922 an orchestral accompaniment was arranged by Sir Edward Elgar. Parry's ashes repose in the crypt of St Paul's Cathedral, London.

AMILCARE PONCHIELLI
(1834–1886)

This Italian composer is mentioned here because of the *Dance of the Hours*, voted by listeners as one of their Hundred Best Tunes. It is the ballet music from the opera *La Gioconda*, the one work upon which Ponchielli's fame rests.

La Gioconda was first performed at La Scala, Milan, in 1876, and hailed by the critics as worthy of ranking with Verdi. It is a spectacle in the true tradition of grand opera, an exciting story of love, jealousy and infamy. The magnificent ballet interlude in the third act, *The Dance of the Hours*, is a representation of the 'eternal struggle between darkness and light'. Aided by dramatic lighting effects, the four sets of dancers are usually dressed as follows: one group in black decorated with silver stars to represent the hours of night; another group in pink, for dawn; the third group in the golden tints of midday; and the last in shades of mauve representing twilight.

GIACOMO PUCCINI

(1858–1924)

'Without melody there is no music, and melody is the one thing that gives life to opera.' So went Puccini's maxim.

When his writing was criticized for not being on a grand enough scale, but within a rather limited design, his answer was: 'I love small things, and the only music I can or will make is that of small things, so long as they are true and full of passion and humanity and touch the heart.'

Puccini was born at Lucca in Italy, and came from a family whose name had been prominent in the town's musical circles for many generations. He was twenty-two before he attended the Royal Conservatory in Milan, where he studied under Ponchielli. This came about largely through a grant from the Queen of Italy, to whom Puccini's mother had applied.

He attracted some attention with his very first opera *Le Villi* ('The Witches'), which he had entered in a competition. Though not one of the prizewinners, it was thought to be of sufficient merit to warrant publication and a performance. With the money he earned—several thousand lire—he considered himself affluent beyond his wildest dreams, a happy state of affairs which was not to last. He maintained himself by giving piano lessons.

Produced at La Scala, his next opera was a failure, but within four years he was to see one of his works accepted in the opera houses of the world. *Manon Lescaut* was presented in Turin in 1893 to such acclaim that Puccini became instantly a composer to be reckoned with. In the ten years that lay ahead, one masterwork succeeded another: *La Bohème, Tosca* and *Madame Butterfly*. This was his greatest and most fruitful period, and in the minds of the Italian people Puccini had donned the mantle that once was Verdi's.

While he was writing *Turandot* in 1924, he became severely ill. It was diagnosed as cancer of the throat. Following an operation he suffered a heart attack and died on 29 November 1924. The news of his death was received with profound shock. At the

Opera House in Rome a performance of *La Bohème* paused while the orchestra played Chopin's *Funeral March*, and the audience stood in homage to his memory.

In his own field Puccini was a master. He composed melodies that enchant the ear and stir the emotions. Opera lovers throughout the world will never tire of what was once referred to as the 'Puccini manner'.

La Bohème. The opera was introduced in Turin in 1896 with Toscanini conducting. Puccini's gorgeous flowing melodies enhance a simple story set in the Latin Quarter of Paris. Considered Puccini's finest score, the most famous numbers are the tenor aria 'Che gelida manina' ('Your tiny hand is frozen'), 'Si mi chiamano Mimi' ('They call me Mimi'), Musetta's Waltz song 'Quando m'en vo', and the beautiful duet at the end of Act I, 'O Soave fanciulla' ('O lovely maid in the moonlight').

Tosca is a tragic opera whose libretto is based on a celebrated play in which the great actress, Sarah Bernhardt, had played the title role. Puccini's score, sombre and dramatic, has given us two of his finest arias. The first is Tosca's prayer to the Virgin, 'Vissi d'arte' ('Art and love, these I have lived for'). 'I have done harm to no one,' she sings. 'Why does the Lord forsake me now?' And then her lover Cavaradossi's poignant farewell. Condemned to death, he is writing his last letter to Tosca, and as he does so his thoughts wander to memories of their past times together in 'E lucevan le stelle' ('When the stars were brightly shining').

Madame Butterfly. When the opera was presented for the first time at La Scala, the audience condemned it outright; there was uproar in the theatre. The crowd hissed and booed, and the music was drowned by the din. In a rage Puccini withdrew his work after this one performance, and three months later a revised version was produced in the provincial town of Brescia. Its overwhelming success there foreshadowed the appreciative welcome it was to receive ever after.

Among the opera's best-known passages are the melodious 'Love Duet' at the end of the first act, the famous aria 'Un bel di vedremo' in which Butterfly visualizes the return of her lover Pinkerton—'One fine day', and the soft chant of the 'Humming Chorus' as, through the night, she watches for him to come ashore.

Turandot. A few words are due about this opera because of its superb tenor aria 'Nessum dorma' ('None shall sleep'), and because of a remarkable and affecting incident at its première.

It was Puccini's last work, left unfinished at the time of his death, completed by Franco Alfano and introduced in 1926 under the baton of Toscanini. In the third act, after Liu had taken her own life, Toscanini stopped the performance, turned to the audience and said: 'It was at this point the master laid down his pen.' With that he left his stand, and the hushed audience quietly filed out of the theatre.

SERGEI RAKHMANINOV
(1873–1943)

While still a student at the Moscow Conservatoire, Rakhmaninov's musical gifts were compared with those of the young Mozart. His creative ability, it was said, bordered on the marvellous. At nineteen he took the Great Gold Medal for composition, the highest award offered by the Conservatoire, and within a year he had written the piano piece that was to pursue and even haunt him for most of his life. Rakhmaninov's Prelude in C Sharp Minor was to become *the* party piece; no respectable music case was complete without it.

In spite of his early achievements, his path was not entirely smooth and he was subject to frequent bouts of despair. He was excessively self-critical, a condition of mind that was worsened when his first symphony was performed to a chorus of condemnation from all quarters. Rimsky-Korsakov told him, 'Forgive me, but I do not find this music at all agreeable', while César Cui mercilessly commented: 'If there was a conservatory in Hell, and if one of the talented pupils had been commissioned to compose a symphony resembling that of Rakhmaninov, he would have brought ecstasy to its inhabitants.' Rakhmaninov blamed the conductor—who on this occasion happened to be Glazunov—for its failure, and added: 'When the indescribable torture of this performance had at last come to an end, I was a different man.'

A factor of considerable importance in Rakhmaninov's early career was his friendship with Tchaikovsky. He tells us: 'To him I owe the first and possibly the deciding success in my life. Tchaikovsky was about fifty-five at the time, that is to say, more than twice my age, but he talked to me, a young beginner, as if I were his equal. He wanted to help me, but he was also anxious not to offend or humiliate me. I soon felt the result of his kindness. Through him I began to be known. . . .'

Following upon this, one of the next steps in his mounting career was as an opera conductor in Moscow, a role he accomplished with the warmest approval of the critics. The next year, 1898, he appeared at a concert in London, enjoying success in the three capacities of composer, pianist and conductor. And, of course, he was not allowed to leave the platform until he had played his Prelude in C Sharp Minor.

He was a prolific composer whose work often reveals the brooding sadness that was so much a part of his character. As a virtuoso pianist Rakhmaninov was famous the world over, drawing large audiences wherever he played.

In 1917, at the time of the revolution, he left Russia and made his home in the United States. When he was getting on in years he said in one of his reflective moods: 'Today when the greater part of my life is over I am constantly troubled by the misgiving that, in venturing into too many fields, I have failed to make the best use of my life. In the old Russian phrase, I have hunted three hares. Can I be sure that I have killed one of them?'

Piano Concerto no. 2 in C Minor. Probably the most popular piano concerto of this century. The circumstances that gave rise to this work are indeed curious. It is dedicated to a Dr Dahl who, by hypnotic means, had cured Rakhmaninov of the paralysing apathy that had possessed him after the dismal failure of his first symphony. The composer has related that as he lay half asleep, day after day for several months he heard the doctor repeat: 'You will begin to write your concerto. You will work with great facility. . . . The concerto will be of excellent quality.' Rakhmaninov said of this: 'Although it may seem incredible, it helped me, and I started to compose again. New musical ideas began to stir within me, far more than I needed for my concerto.' This was the work that set his fame, and he was the soloist at its first performance in Moscow in 1901.

Rhapsody on a Theme of Paganini. Written in 1934, the Rhapsody was Rakhmaninov's most important work after he left Russia. He chose as his theme the Paganini *Caprice* in A Minor. The work is in fact a set of twenty-four variations, of which the eighteenth, a lovely languid piece of music, is renowned and often played on its own. The Rhapsody was used as the musical background for the ballet called *Paganini* which was presented at Covent Garden in 1939, choreographed by Fokine.

Prelude in C Sharp Minor. Many are the explanations invented about this Prelude. What drama lay behind it? What was its deep significance? When Rakhmaninov was asked what inspired him to write it his answer was, 'Forty roubles. I was offered two hundred roubles for five short piano pieces and this was one of them.'

MAURICE RAVEL

(1875–1937)

Ravel was born in Ciboure, on the French side of the Pyrenees, and began to study the piano when he was six. At fourteen he was admitted to the Paris Conservatoire where he spent fifteen years. When, at the end of this time, he was barred from entering for the Prix de Rome, there was an outcry. The press called it a scandal and all of musical Paris took sides. A member of the Prize Committee defiantly asserted that 'Monsieur Ravel may certainly consider us uninspired, but he won't take us for imbeciles with impunity'.

Ravel was not unused to controversy. He had by this time written a number of important compositions in some of which he had been accused of imitating Debussy, and a charge of plagiarism had been levelled against him. How much he had obviously been influenced by Debussy is a matter of opinion. That he played a significant part in the development of modern music cannot be denied. Many people find much of his work rather cold and dry, but as one devotee explained, 'to understand it aright, the listener must be able to put himself in the same emotional mood as that which inspired the composer'.

At the first performance of Ravel's *Rhapsodie Espagnole* a band of his followers in the gallery demanded an encore of one of the movements while the stalls remained unusually cool. One of the enthusiasts shouted to the conductor: 'Play it again for the people downstairs—they haven't understood it!'

That might well apply to other audiences. We may not understand all of his music, but we can and do enjoy the sensationally successful *Boléro*, the charming *Pavane for a Dead Infanta* and the beauty of *Daphnis et Chloé*.

Boléro. This seventeen-minute crescendo—as Ravel himself described it—is built upon a single theme which is repeated over and over again, and is said to be a centuries-old Spanish song.

Ravel did not think very highly of this, his most popular composition, and used to speak of it as 'orchestral effects without music'. It was composed for Ida Rubinstein, the Franco-Russian dancer who introduced it at the Paris opera in 1929. The setting of her dance pantomime was an Andalusian inn frequented by gipsies which, at the start of the music, is empty but for a solitary dancing girl. Ida Rubinstein danced the *Boléro* on a table, her movements slow and sensuous at first, becoming more and more violent as the music increased in intensity, impelling the gipsies entering the inn to join in the dancing. With the music's mounting excitement the floor becomes a mass of whirling figures.

Pavane for a Dead Infanta. This graceful elegy is an arrangement for orchestra of an early piano composition. Although we might expect to look upon it as the dignified and stately dance of a young princess at the court of Spain, Ravel assured his audiences that this pavane might be for any child.

Daphnis et Chloé. Composed for Diaghilev and his Ballet Russe, this was first performed in 1912 when the title roles were created by Nijinsky and Karsavina. Pierre Monteux was the conductor.

The music is best known in the form of two orchestral suites, the second of which contains its most popular excerpt, *Daybreak*, to which Ravel appended this description: 'No sound save the murmur of the brooklets fed by the dew that drips from the rocks. Little by little the day breaks. The birds sing and, afar off, a shepherd passes with his flock . . .'.

NICOLAI RIMSKY-KORSAKOV
(1844–1908)

Rimsky-Korsakov was not formally trained for a musical career but arrived at it after a period in the Russian navy. On his own admission he started as an amateur, much like Mussorgsky who had been an army officer. He came from an aristocratic family to whom the idea of their son being a professional musician was unthinkable.

From the time Rimsky-Korsakov was a small child he showed an unusual interest in music. In his autobiography he mentions that when he was four or five, without sight of the keyboard he could name any note his father sounded on the piano. A little later he started to take piano lessons, and these continued even when he was sent to the naval college at St Petersburg, and he gave as many hours to his music as he could spare. His meeting with Balakirev, who introduced him to the other young musicians who were later to form 'the five', intensified his determination that when the time came, he would devote his life to music.

While on service with the navy he composed his first symphony which was performed under Balakirev in St Petersburg where it was highly praised. Within two years he was to resign from the service and make music his vocation. At twenty-seven, after only a few of his works had been heard, he was, to his astonishment, appointed a professor of composition at the Conservatory. In his own words, 'At the time I could not decently harmonize a chorale . . . and hardly had any notion of the structure of a fugue.' But by dint of hard study he managed to stay one jump ahead of his pupils, and it was now that he started to learn his craft and become one of its most skilful masters.

He remained on the staff of the Conservatory till the end of his life, during which time a whole generation of young composers were directly influenced both by the man and by his music. As a conductor he was significantly responsible for bringing forward their new works to the attention of Russian audiences.

In 1905 he published an open letter to the government, protesting at the presence of armed police at the Conservatory whose job was to suppress student opinion. The students marched to a folk-song called *Dubinushka*, a traditional song of dissent, and when this was banned by the authorities, Rimsky-Korsakov, in sympathy with the student cause, made an orchestral arrangement of it as a gesture of defiance. He was dismissed, and Glazunov, Liadov and others at once resigned. All were later reinstated.

It was once said that Rimsky-Korsakov's three main inspirations were the folksong, the Orient and the sea, all of which are clearly discernible in his immense output which included fifteen operas.

Scheherazade. This symphonic suite after 'The Thousand and One Nights' is unquestionably Rimsky-Korsakov's most popular work. On the score is the following note: 'The Sultan Schahriar, convinced of the faithlessness of women, has sworn to put to death each one of his wives after the first night. But the Sultana Scheherazade saved her life by diverting him with tales which she told him during a thousand and one nights. Overcome by curiosity, the sultan deferred her execution from day to day until at last he renounced his cold-blooded vow.'

The work is a musical illustration of four of the tales, and the violin theme stands for Scheherazade's voice as she begins her stories.

Capriccio Espagnole. Rimsky-Korsakov first sketched this as a 'virtuoso violin fantasy on Spanish themes', but it was revised and evolved finally as the work we know now. At its première in St Petersburg in 1877, under the composer's baton, it was given a great ovation. Even at rehearsal the first movement had hardly finished when the orchestra began to applaud. Tchaikovsky sent congratulations to Rimsky-Korsakov and wrote: 'Your Spanish Caprice is a colossal masterpiece of instrumentation and you may regard yourself as the greatest master of the present day.'

GIOACCHINO ROSSINI
(1792–1868)

Rossini, who wrote thirty-four of his thirty-seven operas within a span of fourteen years, remains one of the enigmas of musical history. The question has been asked many times and though innumerable and varying answers have been put forward we are still left wondering why, at the age of thirty-seven, he suddenly chose to cut himself off almost completely from all musical activity.

Except for his two sacred works, the *Stabat Mater* and the *Mass*, and a few less important vocal and piano pieces, Rossini sat back for the rest of his life and did little more than glory in his past. He died at the age of seventy-six, after thirty-nine latterly unproductive years. He was at the pinnacle of his fame, and his creative ability when he 'retired' was, it seemed, as strong as ever. He could still boast, 'Give me a laundry list and I will set it to music.' The ease with which he composed and the wealth of music that was in him were such that one recalls the oft-repeated story of the time he was writing an opera in bed when a sheet of manuscript fell on the floor. It was too much trouble for him to get out of bed to retrieve it, so he merely wrote the 'missing' part over again!

Why then did he retire? Some say he was too comfortably off to care any more. He could afford to be idle and desired only the good life. He enjoyed adulation, was greatly admired by women and had a fondness for the delights of the table. He once said: 'I would rather be a sausage maker than a composer.' All this is by the way, as the answer obviously lies elsewhere. Did he perhaps feel that he had played himself out? Was he beginning to lose his inspiration? Perhaps the whole truth lies in the statement that he himself is supposed to have made: 'I wrote operas when melodies overwhelmed me, when they came searching for me. But one day I noticed that they did not come any more, that I had to search for them. And that is the moment when I gave it up.'

By his twentieth birthday Rossini had five operas to his credit that had achieved minor success, and he was now ready to storm the citadel. It was not long before he came up with the work that would spread his name beyond Venice and beyond Italy—this was *Tancredi*. The public were overwhelmed by it, and one of its tunes, 'Di tante palpiti', was whistled and sung to such an extent that a court order had to be issued forbidding it in the streets of Venice.

Within three months Rossini won even greater approbation with his comic opera *The Italian Girl in Algiers*. Such scintillating, witty and exciting music was new to them, and the Venetians were again overwhelmed. Rossini now had the world at his feet, and each new opera was enthusiastically welcomed wherever it was performed. *The Barber of Seville*, though it met with mishaps on its first production, immortalized his name.

With his final opera, *William Tell*, Rossini took his last bow from the stage and went into 'retirement'. But he had left his mark on Italian opera. And more: through his lively, sparkling music he had added not a little to the gaiety of nations.

The Barber of Seville. Rossini was compelled to have this opera ready in a fortnight, which meant that he was tempted to, and did, take music from some of his previous works. The Overture, for example, was one he had used in two of his earlier operas.

The first performance in Rome was a disaster. There was an organized demonstration against it, and according to one of the singers, 'hot-headed enemies assembled at their posts as soon as the theatre opened'. There was hissing, apart from which so many things went wrong that the audience was constantly convulsed with laughter. When a tenor had trouble tuning his guitar they collapsed, and later merriment drowned the music when a guitar string broke during a tender aria. In the middle a singer's nose started to bleed, and to crown it all, when a cat walked slowly and unconcernedly across the stage, the audience became quite uncontrollable.

Fortunately, the second performance was an enormous success, and the opera has held its own ever since. The Overture and its two famous numbers—Figaro's 'Largo al factotum' and the soprano song 'Una voce poco fa' ('A voice heard just now')—are tunes the whole world knows.

William Tell. Rossini intended this, his last opera, to be his masterpiece. First performed in Paris it was a considerable success at the time and lavishly praised but has failed to hold the public's esteem. Its Overture, however, achieved world-wide fame and has been called a complete symphonic poem in miniature.

The Thieving Magpie. Finally, a brief note about *La Gazza Ladra* ('The Thieving Magpie'), which was a milestone in Rossini's career. It contained new ideas and much excellent music but, like so many of his other operas, only the Overture is at all well known. As one of the hundred best tunes, it is perhaps more popular today than ever.

CAMILLE SAINT-SAËNS
(1835–1921)

Saint-Saëns was a very remarkable man indeed. At times during his life he was compared to both Mozart and Beethoven, and his massive output remains unequalled in French music. As he once remarked, 'I produce music as the apple tree produces apples'. His is not a name that trips off the tongue as do others much less interesting, and yet only to mention *The Carnival of Animals*, *Danse Macabre*, *Le Rouet d'Omphale*, the opera *Samson and Delilah*, and his piece for violin and orchestra *Introduction and Rondo Capriccioso*, apart from his beguiling piano concertos and symphonies, is to begin to make your listener aware of the magnitude of this composer's popular achievement.

Saint-Saëns was a child phenomenon, second perhaps only to Mozart in the precocious musical gift he exhibited in his early years. He was hardly two years old when he began piano lessons, and at five he made his public bow with a violinist in a Beethoven Sonata. It is said that at this age too he played a Grétry opera from the score. His was a rare talent and his advance so rapid that long before he was ten he gave a piano recital at the best concert hall in Paris in a programme that included Handel, Bach and Beethoven. By the time he had entered the Conservatoire at thirteen, his compositions were known in Paris musical circles, but he was turned down for the Prix de Rome, Berlioz being one who voted against him. His reason was that 'Saint-Saëns knows everything but lacks melody'; he was always to encounter as many enemies as defenders. As a critic observed after hearing one of his pieces, 'That's certainly bad music, but it's well written'. In 1857 he became the organist at the famous Church of the Madeleine in Paris, one of the most enviable of appointments. He excelled as an organist and pianist, and his keyboard technique was brilliant. Wagner recalled being simply stunned by his prodigious skill—especially when he played the whole of *Tristan und Isolde* from memory.

In addition to his many musical activities, Saint-Saëns was a scholar of the keenest intellect—a mathematician of a very high order, an astronomer of reputation, a linguist and the possessor of a wide knowledge of classical literature. He was a very remarkable man.

Samson and Delilah. This is Saint-Saëns's most famous work, which faithfully reproduces the Old Testament story from the Book of Judges. The Paris Opéra repeatedly rejected it, considering it to be too advanced and in the Wagnerian mould. It was left to Franz Liszt to give it its first performance at Weimar in 1877, but not for another fifteen years did it reach Paris and a triumphant reception. For many years thereafter it was featured regularly each season. Among its outstanding pages are the contralto aria 'Mon Cœur S'ouvre à ta voix ('Softly awakes my heart') and the *Bacchanale.*

The Carnival of Animals. The composer termed these descriptive pieces 'A Grand Zoological Fantasy', but after a private performance in 1887 he forbade public presentation as he considered it nothing more than a musical joke. The only part he permitted to be played was the now famous melody that represents the swan, a graceful and tranquil piece originally written for a 'cello and two pianos which has since been heard in arrangements of every kind. Only after Saint-Saens's death was the prohibition removed by a clause in his will. There are fourteen sections in the suite characterizing different animals in a pungent, brilliant manner. The eighth section, *Personages with Long Ears*, is taken to be a dig at the music critics.

Danse Macabre. Saint-Saëns wrote four symphonic poems of which this is the most popular, but its first audience thought it in very poor taste. He based his work on some French verses of the same title, and after setting the words to music abandoned the idea in favour of an orchestral piece that depicts 'Death playing a dance tune on his violin at midnight. . . . White skeletons run and leap about in their shrouds, their bones rattling as the dance gets wilder and wilder, until the crowing of the cock tells them that dawn has come and the ghostly merry-making must end.'

FRANZ SCHUBERT

(1797–1828)

Melody flowed from Schubert, the 'prince of lyricists', as the scent from a rose.

He was born in Vienna, the youngest son of a parish school-master and had eighteen brothers and sisters, few of whom lived very long. His father and two brothers began to teach him music, but found that Franz had somehow mastered the rudiments him-self. When the choirmaster of the local church then took him in hand, he too observed that 'whenever I wanted to teach him any-thing, he knew it already'.

At eleven Schubert gained an entrance to the Convict School which trained choristers for the Imperial Court Chapel. It was also a sort of free grammar school where poor students were boarded gratuitously. His unusual talent was quickly recognized and brought to the attention of Salieri who was then considered Mozart's rival, with the recommendation that 'the lad seems to have been taught by God himself. He seems to know everything'.

Salieri took the boy under his own wing and had to admit that Schubert was a born genius who could do whatever he chose. Even at the tender age of thirteen his musical output was enormous. Symphonies, songs and quartets—all were forthcoming in a steady flow, and were performed at the Convict Academy. When he left there Schubert took to teaching at his father's school; but he cared little about his pupils, being too preoccupied with composition. The stream of music was unceasing. The year 1815 was probably his most prolific year, and witnessed the production of over one hundred and forty songs, five operas, several symphonies, two masses and other church and chamber music. Despite all this, while he did indeed have a small group of admirers, he was comparatively unknown to the general public. No publisher showed any interest in his work, and it remained for his friends to set up a fund in order to have some of his compositions brought to publication. Yet this did nothing to ease his wretched poverty, earning him a mere pittance.

Schubert had gathered round him a small but congenial circle of friends. They were very close to him and their comradeship endured to the end of his life. His only moments of happiness were in their company, whether it was in the cafés or at the musical evenings they frequently held. One of his friends, a poet called Schober, is remembered for the lines inscribed on Schubert's coffin beginning 'All Bliss be Thine, Thou pure angelic soul'.

For thirty years, although Schubert and Beethoven had lived in the same city they had never met; Schubert worshipped the older man at a distance. 'Who,' he exclaimed, 'could hope to do anything after Beethoven?' At their first meeting Beethoven, being quite deaf, requested Schubert to write down his answers. The young man's hand shook so much from nervousness that he could say nothing and he left, covered in confusion. When Beethoven was dying Schubert visited him and stood gazing at the master in silence for some while, then suddenly burst into tears and hurried from the room.

With the passing years Schubert became extremely unhappy and sank into deepest despondency. In 1824 he wrote to a friend:

'Every night when I go to sleep I hope that I may never wake again, and every morning renews the grief of yesterday. My affairs are going badly, I never have any money. . . .' No doubt he suffered from exhaustion. He had been crossed in love, but above all he considered himself a failure. In the last years of his life his health had been failing and yet he did not relax and composed some of his finest works during this time. When at last recognition was coming his way, and was even within his grasp, ill health and disappointment took their toll and he died before he was thirty-two. He was buried near Beethoven, and the inscription on the plinth beneath his bust reads: 'Music buried here a rich treasure, and yet more glorious hopes.'

Symphony no. 8 in B Minor (*Unfinished*). In 1822 Schubert was elected an honorary member of a music society in Graz, and as a mark of gratitude said he would present them with one of his symphonies. After two full movements and nine bars of a third were written, he decided to submit it to them unfinished. He entrusted the score to a friend to deliver, but for some inexplicable reason it never arrived. Though its existence was known to a handful of people, its whereabouts was not brought to light until 1865, when a well-known Viennese conductor was apprised of it and discovered the manuscript in the possession of the very friend to whom Schubert had handed it such a long time before. Thus, thirty-seven years after Schubert's death, this great symphony received its first performance. Why it was never completed, or why his friend withheld it, have been the subjects of much speculation, but no satisfactory answers have so far been advanced.

Rosamunde: Incidental Music. *Rosamunde* was a drama presented at the Theater-an-der-Wien in 1823. It ran for two nights and then disappeared into the limbo of forgotten things. Schubert's charming incidental music suffered a similar fate.

Over forty years later, and suspecting that a wealth of Schubert music lay hidden away, George Grove of the famous *Dictionary of Music* and the young Arthur Sullivan went on a journey of discovery to Vienna. There in a publishing house, amid heaps of old manuscripts and other neglected, dusty and yellowing material, they came upon all the lost parts of *Rosamunde* and much other music. It is recorded that in sheer delight the two men played a jubilant game of leap-frog round the room.

Quintet in A Major (*The Trout*). Perhaps the best known to the general public of all Schubert's chamber works, *The Trout* Quintet was composed in 1819 while he was on holiday with friends in Upper Austria. It was probably written for an informal evening of music-making, and it is thought that Schubert's host suggested that he compose something for the small group, incorporating his song 'Die Forelle' ('The Trout'). The fourth of the five movements is a set of variations on the song.

The unusual combination of instruments—violin, viola, 'cello, double bass and piano—might hint at the variety of musicians in the party.

Schubert composed over six hundred songs, many of them masterpieces, but in selecting the few that the space of this book allows, I must lean towards those most frequently asked for.

'Erl King'. Sitting alone in his room one day in 1815, Schubert happened to take up a volume of Goethe's poems and read the 'Erl King'. The rushing sound and the stress of the storm became for him immediate realities, and in a state of extreme excitement he sketched the ballad and rushed to a piano to play it through. One of his great inspirations, it was only published six years later when his friend Vogl, a fine baritone, made it popular.

'Ave Maria'

> *. . . Safe may we sleep beneath Thy care,*
> *Though banished, outcast, and reviled;*
> *Maiden! hear a maiden's prayer—*
> *Mother, hear a suppliant child!*
> *Ave Maria!*

In 1825 Schubert referred to 'Ave Maria' in a letter to his father
in which he spoke of a musical evening: 'My new songs from
Walter Scott's *Lady of the Lake* especially had much success. They
also wondered greatly at my piety, which I expressed in a hymn to
the Holy Virgin and which, it appears, grips every soul and turns
it to devotion.'

The 'Ave Maria' was one of seven songs set by Schubert from
Lady of the Lake. It is the prayer of Ellen Douglas, the poem's
fair young heroine, heard at evening on Lake Katrine.

'Ständchen' ('Serenade'). No song of Schubert's is more widely
admired or known than this. It comes from a set of fourteen songs
with the title of *Schwanengesang* ('Swan Song'), so named by a
publisher after Schubert's death. Composed in his last year, this
collection can thus literally be called Schubert's 'Swan Song'. It
is without doubt one of the most beautiful love songs ever
written.

Die Winterreise ('The Winter Journey'). This cycle of twenty-four
songs was said to have affected Schubert more than any others he
had written. When his friends criticized their sombre mood he
replied: 'These songs please me more than all the rest, and in time
they will please you as well.' Later his friends agreed that he was
right, for they too became enthusiastic about these sorrowful
melodies which tell of a distracted lover who, in his overwhelming grief, takes to the lonely winter road. The songs describe his
thoughts and his encounters on the way. 'Der Lindenbaum'
('The Lime Tree') was the favourite of the cycle with Schubert's
friends when they first heard it, retaining this popularity with
present-day listeners.

ROBERT SCHUMANN
(1810–1856)

As a boy Schumann was torn between the opposing views of his parents as to his future. His mother was averse to her son's musical ambitions, while his father looked kindly on the boy's wishes, and even went so far as to approach Carl Maria Weber to take him as a pupil.

Unfortunately Schumann senior died when Robert was fifteen, and it was his mother who decided on a career for him. It was to be the law. So at eighteen he was sent to Leipzig University. But it was little law he studied as he became more determined than ever to adopt music as a profession. In Leipzig he took lessons from Friedrich Wieck, who soon became aware of Schumann's talent and persuaded his mother to relent.

Schumann applied himself somewhat overzealously to the piano, and in the rash use of an apparatus to improve his technique, he seriously damaged his right hand, which destroyed his dream of being a virtuoso, and established that composing was to be his life's work.

For Schumann 1834 was an important year. He was the editor of a new music journal that was to become famous in the annals of musical history. The *Neue Zeitschrift für Musik* was born of his idealism and that of his friends who forgathered each evening 'to exchange ideas on the art which was to them meat and drink, namely music'. For many years the journal exerted a powerful influence on the trend of music in Germany.

The next milestone in Schumann's life was his love for Clara Wieck, a brilliant pianist and the daughter of his former teacher. But her father was resolute in preventing any alliance between them, and for long periods it was impossible for them to meet. Instead Schumann voiced his love through his music. When, at concerts, she played a sonata he had dedicated to her, it was his 'unique cry of passion'. Finally, after four clouded years, their hearts' desire was attained (but only through recourse to a court of law) when they were granted permission to marry.

One of the happy consequences of his new life was that he 'burst into song' for the first time. In the year of his marriage he poured out no fewer than a hundred and thirty of his finest songs in which he expressed his every emotion, and in the several years following he worked to the full limit of his powers. He also composed two symphonies. The first, the *Spring* Symphony, under Mendelssohn's direction was received very well. With his chamber music, of which his piano quintet is considered a masterpiece, he was beginning to reach a wider audience.

In 1844, however, he had a mental breakdown, and retired more and more into himself. 'I suffer very much from my nerves and everything affects and exhausts me,' he wrote. But in a year or so he had recovered sufficiently to resume composition with much of his earlier vigour. He was in fact more prolific than ever. He completed his famous piano concerto, two further symphonies and a deal of music of all kinds.

But there were still intermittent periods of depression, and eventually his mental distress reached its crisis when he attempted suicide by throwing himself from a bridge into the Rhine. His life was saved, but he was taken and confined in a private asylum, where he died two years later.

Only near the end was Clara allowed to visit him. For a while he sat and gazed at her. Slowly a look of recognition came into his eyes. He reached for her hand and held it to him, and then gently he took her in his arms.

Clara said later: 'For all the world's treasures, I would not give the memory of this one embrace.'

Piano Concerto in A Minor. When the first movement was complete—Schumann had not intended it as part of a concerto—he called it a *Fantasie* (in A Minor) and for some years it was played as a single piece under a number of different titles. When two further movements were added in 1845, and the work was finally launched as a concerto, it was still not a great success.

When Clara introduced the concerto to London in 1856, one critic wrote of 'her praiseworthy efforts to make her husband's curious rhapsody pass for music'. But tastes do indeed change, and today it ranks as one of the world's favourite piano concertos.

Träumerei ('dreaming' or 'reverie') is a classic, a charming miniature that comes from *Kinderscenen* ('Scenes from Childhood'), a set of thirteen piano pieces which were not written for children but are, rather, Schumann's views of a child's world. He gave a title to each of these little pieces, thus indicating the various aspects he wished to portray.

Die Beiden Grenadiere ('The Two Grenadiers'). In this dramatic ballad Heine's poetry and Schumann's melody are not distinct and separate elements but indivisible parts. Each has contributed equally to produce a truly wonderful song that tells of two French soldiers returning wearily to their homeland from the battlefields of Russia when they learn of the defeat of France and the captivity of the emperor. One of the grenadiers has been wounded and begs that, should he die now, his comrade will see that he is laid in French earth, so that he can silently listen and one day again answer his emperor's call.

Serenata

Serenata by Toselli. Enrico Toselli (1883–1926), an Italian pianist, was seventeen when he composed this internationally successful piece of music in 1901. Apart from the *Serenata* his music is less well known than his elopement and marriage with the Crown Princess Luisa of Saxony.

JEAN SIBELIUS
(1865–1957)

Finland's 'Grand Old Man', Sibelius, was a legend in his own country during his lifetime. He was a national hero and the Finns were proud that, through his musical attainments, their 'little' country had found a place in the larger cultural world. No Finn was ever so revered.

In his early youth Sibelius had shown some aptitude for the violin, and had even composed a few small pieces. Professionally it was intended that he should follow the legal profession and, with this in mind, he entered the University of Helsinki. After a year, however, he found legal studies disagreeable and was certain that he could only be happy if he concentrated whole-heartedly on music, his one absorbing interest.

When he was twenty-four he was awarded a government grant that enabled him to travel abroad for further musical study. In Berlin and Vienna, two of the world's music capitals, he was awakened to fresh horizons that would shape his whole future. His creative work assumed new proportions, and when he returned to his native country it was not long before he began to acquire the beginnings of a notable reputation. His first important composition was *En Saga*, a tone poem for orchestra which was immediately recognized as a work of immense talent.

Sibelius, married with a child expected, had somehow to augment his income, so he became a teacher at the Music Institute in Helsinki. He had already composed the *Karelia* Suite and the *Lemminkainen Suite* from which comes *The Swan of Tuonela*. In 1897 the state once again rewarded him with a stipend to make him financially free, so it was now possible for him to devote his time to composition.

In the following few short years he made his mark with *Finlandia* and his first symphony among a host of works in various forms. Sibelius was a composer of national music that represented the voice of his people. He was imbued with a strong sense of patriotism, and was directly influenced by the ancient legends of his race. His love of the Finnish landscape is reflected in much of his work and expresses its cold sombre beauty.

His seven symphonies and his tone poems attest to his formidable position in twentieth-century music. No other composer ever lived to enjoy as many honours as were bestowed upon him by his people. When he died their feelings were indicated by a Helsinki newspaper when it said: 'Sibelius is the last of Finland's great men. It will be a long time before we have another.'

Finlandia. Unquestionably the most famous of Sibelius's works, this tone poem was composed in 1899 at a time when Finland was oppressed by the Russians. This was the music for the finale of a series of six dramatic tableaux illustrating Finnish history. Performed at a fund-raising campaign in Helsinki it was then called *Finland Awakes.* Its impact was so immediately effective and roused audiences to such a fever pitch that it became symbolic of the defiant voice of the people. The following year it was renamed *Finlandia*, and is a more patriotic symbol to the Finns than their national anthem.

The Swan of Tuonela. This is the third section of the *Lemminkainen* Suite, four 'Legends' adapted for orchestra and based on stories in the *Kalevala*, an ancient Finnish epic.

A preface to the score reads: 'Tuonela, the Kingdom of Death and Hades of Finnish mythology, is surrounded by a broad river of black water and rapid current, on which the Swan of Tuonela glides in majestic fashion and sings.'

Karelia Suite is one of his early works, taken from a much larger score written for seven tableaux representing historical aspects of Karelia, in south-eastern Finland. Sibelius chose the best numbers with which to build this suite, the most popular movement being the third, the cheerful *Alla Marcia*.

Valse Triste. In 1903 Sibelius composed some incidental music for a play called *Kuolema* ('Death'), written by his brother-in-law, Arvid Järnefelt. The play was a failure, and would have remained forgotten but for this one piece of music. The *Valse Triste* is a dreamy waltz tune that accompanies the last dance of a woman who has risen from her death-bed. It was little thought of at the time, but with publication it soon became known all over Europe.

'The Skaters' Waltz'

This is the best-known composition of Emil Waldteufel (1837–1915), who was born in Strasbourg and studied at the Paris Conservatoire. The success of his first waltzes prompted him to devote himself wholly to writing dance music. He toured the capitals of Europe with an orchestra which played his own dance tunes of which he composed over two hundred and fifty. He became known as the 'French Strauss', and was for a time the court musician to the Empress Eugénie. Another of his popular pieces is *Estudiantina*.

JOHANN STRAUSS II

(1825–1899)

When Vienna waltzed the Strauss family supplied the music, a habit which began a hundred and fifty years ago in the time of Johann Strauss the elder. By 1849, according to a contemporary, Strauss had 'conquered the world'. 'Strauss,' he said, 'is the most popular musician on earth. His waltzes enchant the Americans, they are heard across the Chinese Wall and they resound in

African bivouacs.' Wagner called him a 'demon of the ancient Viennese folk spirit', and a demon he was. What is more, he wanted no son of his to follow in his footsteps—and he had three who survived him.

For his son Johann he had planned a post in a bank. But Frau Strauss, whom he had deserted for another woman, had other ideas. She had made up her mind that young Johann would be more famous than his father. So she saw to his musical education, and at nineteen he was ready to make his début as a conductor at Dommayer's Garden Restaurant. To this end he recruited an orchestra, and posters all over Vienna announced 'the first appearance of Johann Strauss (son), who will have the honour to conduct his own orchestra. In addition to overtures and opera melodies, he will play several of his own compositions. . . . Johann Strauss junior respectfully commends himself to the grace and favour of the public. . . .'

When Johann appeared, the clique sent by his father to disrupt the proceedings placed themselves in front of the orchestra, but their shouts were soon silenced by the extraordinary enthusiasm of the thousands there. It was too crowded for the tables to be occupied, nor was anybody able to dance. But each of his own new numbers had to be repeated time and time again, and his final waltz was encored, believe it or not, eighteen times.

With his striking personality and his good looks, the younger Johann soon became the talk of the café house public. When his father died five years later, it was he who was 'king'. He had no rival. There was something about his playing that was different. He gave his waltzes a quality that audiences had not heard before, and they said of the young Strauss that his music could speak of ecstasy, pain, joy and suffering, all to the lilting rhythm of the waltz. Each new tune that he introduced was greeted with howls of delight, and Vienna developed what was called a 'Strauss madness'. The great composers of the day came to hear him, and Brahms was known to have remarked: 'You must go to the Volksgarten every Friday when Johann Strauss conducts.' Wagner and Verdi were no less complimentary, and for fifty years Johann Strauss reigned. Even when he was seventy, he could still boast that 'the melodies gush out like fresh water'.

He was married three times, but it was his first wife Jetty who inspired his greatest waltzes. It was she too who encouraged him to write for the theatre. With *Die Fledermaus* and *The Gipsy Baron*, Strauss took his place with the immortals of operetta.

138

When he died it was the end of an epoch and seemed as if the soul of Vienna had died with him. The news came during a concert at the Volksgarten, where Strauss himself had so often conducted. Suddenly, as if shocked, the orchestra stopped, and when they resumed playing, it was the *Blue Danube*, solemn and quiet. Then the concert ended.

The *Blue Danube* Waltz

> *Once again my heart's a bower*
> *Shelt'ring blossoms sweet and new;*
> *Arid shrubs burst into flower,*
> *Nightingales all singing too*
> *By the Danube, beautiful blue Danube.*

As Eduard Jacob says in his book on Johann Strauss, 'Who had ever seen the Danube blue? It is a pale green, reed-coloured river, sometimes grey, often silvery and never blue.' But it was to these lines by Karl Beck that Strauss set his music at the request of the Viennese Men's Choral Association. It was to be their big number at a charity performance in 1867. Even with a choir of twelve hundred voices the song made little impression, and Strauss himself seemed not particularly concerned with the failure of one waltz. But after it was heard in Paris six months later, without the choral appendage, its fame spread like wildfire: the rest is history.

Tales from the Vienna Woods. It would perhaps be true to say that this is the second best known of the Strauss waltzes. One outstanding feature is its symphonic introduction which creates an enchanting mood picture. It is the prelude to a flow of rich melody. One of its main themes had been used earlier by Strauss the elder. Johann was obviously very fond of it because he utilized it on two other occasions as well, investing it each time with an individuality of its own.

Roses from the South. In 1880 Strauss composed his operetta entitled *The Queen's Lace Handkerchief*. The plot was a complicated story of royal intrigue set in sixteenth-century Portugal. Surprisingly, much of its music was in waltz tempo. More surprising, it was one of the popular light operas of the day. Nevertheless Strauss rescued some of its best tunes and put them together in a pot-pourri that he called, for some unknown reason, *Roses from the South*. He dedicated it to King Humbert of Italy. Altogether an international affair!

Die Fledermaus. Long famous for his café house dance music, Strauss, in this classic model of an operetta, now successfully brought its gaiety and sparkle into the theatre. But instead of coffee it was champagne.

Based on a French farce, the libretto so fascinated him that he feverishly set to work on the music, shutting himself away from all but his wife until the score was completed. It was introduced in 1874, at a time when the country had been plunged into economic disaster. The stock exchange had crashed and Vienna could hardly have been in a mood to receive it, so its triumph was all the more remarkable.

The *Nuns' Chorus* from *Casanova*. This is included here because, of all Strauss music, it has been highest in the listeners' poll. Calling itself an operetta, *Casanova* is made up of Strauss tunes set to a book described as a story of love and adventure. When the English version was produced at the London Coliseum in 1932, the *Nuns' Chorus* was an instant hit. It was rather facetiously said that 'the nuns were at their devotions to three-four time'. A delicious tune, none the less, it has retained its great popularity these forty years or more.

SIR ARTHUR SULLIVAN

(1842–1900)

It was one of the vagaries of Sullivan's life that the works by which he wanted to be remembered, and upon which he pinned his greatest hopes, have passed into oblivion, while the music that he regarded so lightly and which made him rich and famous, has prevailed as no such music has ever done.

Rarely heard today are the orchestral pieces—his 'serious' works—upon which his early reputation rested. These include *The Tempest* (his first success), the Cello Concerto, the *Irish* Symphony and the *In Memoriam* Overture, which was his cry of grief at the loss of his father. These, as Percy M. Young wrote in his admirable biography of Sullivan, acclaimed him 'the white hope of English music'.

How many of us know anything of *The Light of the World*, an oratorio that was talked of at the time in the same breath as *Messiah* and which, when first given at the Birmingham Festival of 1873, was fully expected to emulate *Elijah*, which Mendelssohn had introduced there a quarter of a century before? Or *The Golden Legend*, dubbed Sullivan's 'queen of cantatas' which he composed within twelve months of *The Mikado*? Of the performance of *The Golden Legend* at the Leeds Festival of 1886 a newspaper wrote: 'Such a frenzy of congratulations has surely never before rung in the ears of any living man, as that amid which Sir Arthur left the platform.' One could name several more like *The Martyr of Antioch* or *The Prodigal Son*, called 'scholarly works' and beloved of the Victorians but now dead.

Of his church music, which Sullivan started to write as a boy of thirteen, only 'Onward Christian Soldiers' survives. But there was a time when he was more renowned for his songs than his operettas. Except for 'The Lost Chord', however, and a recent revival of 'The Long Day Closes', none of over a hundred song compositions is heard nowadays. This then was the paradox of his career.

Arthur Sullivan was born in London, the second son of a bandmaster at the Royal Military College at Sandhurst, who later became a teacher at the Military School of Music, Kneller Hall. It was natural that in such an environment, as he once said, music was the only thing which meant anything to him. By the time he was twelve he was proficient at most of the wind instruments in the band and, furthermore, he possessed a beautiful voice with which he was able to realize one of his young ambitions, to become a chorister of the Chapel Royal at St James's Palace. He was admitted there when he was nine years old. In time he sang solos, and on a number of occasions he was the soloist in anthems of his own composition.

At fourteen, while still at the Chapel Royal, he was awarded the newly founded Mendelssohn scholarship to the Royal Academy of Music. After two years of this he went to Leipzig, acknowledged then to be the foremost conservatory in Europe, where he was a fellow pupil of Grieg. Sullivan was a brilliant student, and in 1861, at the final concert, he conducted his own suite, *The Tempest*, composed as music for Shakespeare's play, and according to the critics heartily applauded. He had made an impression that augured well for his future.

When he returned home there was, of course, the necessity to maintain himself, and he became the organist at the fashionable London church of St Michael's, Chester Square, at eighty pounds a year. The vicar's daughter later wrote that she remembered the slim, curly headed, black eyed youth who enthralled her with his performance of the E Minor Fugue by Bach when he went to show his paces in order to obtain the post.

When Sullivan was twenty-five, and had just had his Symphony in E Flat (*Irish*) performed with great success, he stepped out of character and demonstrated that he was also capable of writing comic music of the best kind. This was for an operetta, *Cox and Box*, which, though originally composed for a private performance—at which George du Maurier played Box—was later transferred to the St George's Hall, where it had a long run. On the same bill was a short play by W. S. Gilbert, but the two men were not destined to meet for another three years, by which time Sullivan had established himself as the leading English composer. When eventually they did come together, they collaborated on a comic opera called *Thespis* which, however, failed to draw much attention, and each went his own way. In 1875 Sullivan was called on by Richard D'Oyly Carte to supply the music for a piece that Gilbert had written on the subject of a breach of promise. The result was *Trial by Jury*.

This began an association which, except for several short intervals, lasted for eleven years. From *HMS Pinafore* to *The Gondoliers* there was an unbroken collaboration between two men who disliked each other intensely, who were always quarrelling, and who never met when away from the theatre. Their union finally ended in 1896 with the production of *The Grand Duke* which, by all accounts, was so bad that it was hard to believe it was the work of the famous partnership. Sullivan's work with other librettists which came after this was hardly more successful. It was an unhappy end to a brilliant and distinguished career.

He was knighted for his services to English music. He had walked with kings, he was rich and lived in luxurious style. He had indeed lived a full life. When he died the whole nation mourned, and *The Times* said in its obituary notice, 'the whole of the Empire was plunged in gloom'. He was buried in St Paul's Cathedral, and on the first anniversary of his death there was a memorial concert at the Queen's Hall. Among the works performed were *In Memoriam* and *The Golden Legend*. As Percy Young has so aptly observed, 'This was the last grand flourish to suggest that Sullivan was a great "serious" composer.'

The Gondoliers (or *The King of Barataria*) was first presented in December 1889 and ran for 554 performances. Earlier that year Sullivan had been to Venice, and it was a pleasing coincidence to learn that Gilbert was thinking of using a Venetian setting for their next 'entirely original comic opera'. A brilliant first night hailed it as one of the happiest pieces ever produced by the celebrated duo. *The Gondoliers* employs the familiar comic plot of mistaken identity, and the scene moves between Venice and the imaginary island of Barataria. Of the songs, 'Take a Pair of Sparkling Eyes' is one of Sullivan's most famous tunes.

The Mikado (or *The Town of Titipu*). *Princess Ida*, running at the Savoy in 1884, was not doing as well as had been expected, and D'Oyly Carte needed a replacement as soon as possible. The fact that there was at the time a wide interest in things Japanese may have had something to do with the choice of subject for the next opera. There was also on exhibition in Knightsbridge a Japanese village, although Gilbert asserted that the hint in fact came from a Japanese executioner's sword hanging on his library wall.

The Mikado opened in March 1885 to prove the greatest success at the Savoy Theatre of any Gilbert and Sullivan opera so far. Somebody once referred to it as 'the tragic Madame Butterfly's comic opera twin'. From a marvellous score I need only mention the 'Wandering Minstrel', 'The Flowers that Bloom in the Spring', the 'Tit Willow' song and 'Three Little Maids from School are We'.

Iolanthe (or *The Peer and The Peri*). 'A census of Sullivan's most studious admirers would probably reveal *Iolanthe* in first place as the finest creation of England's most distinguished musician of the nineteenth century,' wrote Eric Hodgins. Sullivan's delightful music was so popular in fact that on one day alone ten thousand vocal scores were sold.

Iolanthe represents a sly joke at the expense of the peerage, being a fanciful tale of fairies from Arcady invading the solemn portals of the House of Lords. Its first performance was at the newly built Savoy Theatre in 1882, and two of its songs which immediately appealed were 'When I went to the Bar' and the March of the Peers, 'Loudly let the trumpets bray'.

'The Lost Chord'. Though scoffers have tended to denigrate the song, it was a heart-felt expression of Sullivan's sorrow at the death of his brother in 1877. Sullivan was at his bedside, and to ease the hours of a night-long vigil he read some verses by Adelaide Proctor. It was the poem 'The Lost Chord' that stayed in his mind, the setting of which was to make it one of the most famous of all Victorian ballads.

PETER ILYICH TCHAIKOVSKY
(1840–1893)

It is recorded that Tchaikovsky, when no more than five years old, would sometimes be found crying hysterically after listening to music. When asked what was troubling him he would reply, pointing to his head at the same time: 'It is here, the music, it won't leave me.' The strange effect that music had on the highly strung child was but a symptom of the neurosis that was to manifest itself throughout his life. It is scarcely believable, but according to a life-long friend of his, when Tchaikovsky conducted a new work at the Conservatoire he suffered such appalling fright that he used his right hand only, while his left hand supported his chin, terrified that his head might fall off!

At an early age he had shown an unusual musical aptitude. But he, like a number of other great composers in their youth, was made to study law. He was given piano lessons and worked assiduously, but was discouraged from thinking of music as a future. His father at one time questioned his teacher as to whether Peter should exchange law for music, and the answer was a firm 'No'. So he became instead a civil servant at the Ministry of Justice. When he was twenty-two, however, he enrolled at the Conservatoire at St Petersburg, telling his sister: 'Do not for a moment think I expect ever to be a great artist. Whether I become a famous composer or a poor music teacher is a matter of indifference to me. At all events my conscience will be clear, and I shall no longer have the right to complain about my lot.' He graduated with a high award and the recommendation from Anton Rubinstein for the post of teacher of harmony at the Moscow Conservatoire. From now on he was able to devote himself whole-heartedly to composition.

The effort he exerted on his first symphony brought about a nervous breakdown that lasted for several horrifying months, and he was on the brink of insanity. When he recovered, his work began to flow with ease. His first symphony, though initially coldly received, was revised and then performed with great success. Within a further nine years his tally of compositions was an impressive one by any standards. The Fantasy Overture *Romeo and Juliet*, two more symphonies, the first piano concerto, the music for *Swan Lake* and four operas had by now given him a firm reputation. Despite these successes he was always in financial difficulties, the worry of which often hampered his work.

There came now into his life two women, each of whom was to play a momentous part in his future, as a man and as a composer. The first was a pupil at the Conservatoire, Antonina Milyukova. She had been writing him love letters confessing that she had worshipped him at a distance and was his slave, and she begged for nothing more than to meet him. In the beginning Tchaikovsky ignored her letters, but her pleas persisted and her impassioned declarations of love began to disturb him. She even threatened suicide if he disregarded her appeals. Eventually, more out of pity than anything else, he agreed to meet her. He told her that he was grateful for her admiration, that there could never be a relationship between them, and that he could not meet her again. But Antonina was determined, and further meetings did take place, with the result that the simple-hearted Tchaikovsky succumbed to her wiles and proposed marriage.

All attempts by his brother and friends to persuade him to break the engagement failed. He now felt it an obligation and a matter of honour. Within two months he was married. Living with Antonina proved to be a mortifying experience, and one night, after only a few weeks of their life together, Tchaikovsky was unable to bear it any longer and aimlessly wandered the streets in a state of collapse until he found himself at the Moscow river. Hoping to end his misery he walked into the icy water, but was seen and brought out. He was desperately ill, but after a long rest recovered and 'returned to life'. He was forbidden by his doctor to have any further contact with Antonina. In the event, it turned out that she was mentally more ill than he, and twenty of her last years were spent in an institution.

With Nadezhda von Meck he entered upon what was called 'the most amazing romance in musical history'. She was a wealthy, cultured widow who had long admired his music. When she learned of his precarious financial state, she commissioned him to arrange several of his pieces for violin and piano for her own use, and she paid him more than handsomely. Not long afterwards she wrote that she intended to give him a 'pension' of six thousand roubles a year, which would free him from anxiety.

Thus began an association that lasted thirteen years during which, at her sole wish, they never personally met. 'The more fascinating you are to me, the more I am afraid of making your acquaintance,' she wrote. Their friendship was carried on entirely by correspondence in which they confided their innermost thoughts and poured out their hearts in letters which, at times, contained ardent and even passionate expressions of their regard for each other. But thirteen years for such a relationship is a long time and in 1890 the end came. Tchaikovsky heard from her that the annual allowance was to cease. The reason she gave was discovered later to be a pretext, and she concluded her letter: 'Goodbye, my incomparable friend, do not forget one whose love for you is infinite.' To Tchaikovsky it was a bitter disappointment. Not that he needed her money. He was now financially secure and a world-famous composer. Though Madame von Meck did not reply to any of his inquiring letters, he refused to believe that the pen-friendship had become tedious to her, and that the whole affair had been nothing more than the whim of a rich and eccentric patron.

Tchaikovsky lived for three more years to enjoy the fruits of his labours. His music was loved wherever it was played, and tributes came to him from all quarters. In his last year Cambridge University honoured him with a doctorate of music, and when he came to England for the degree ceremony he conducted one of his works at a Royal Philharmonic Concert to an enthusiastic reception. He had just completed his sixth symphony and was wholly delighted with it, and he told a friend that never had he felt so well and happy.

On 2 November 1893, sitting at luncheon with his brother, he refused all food and complained of feeling unwell, asking only for a glass of water. Despite warnings of the danger of cholera, the water he drank was unboiled. That same night he was desperately ill and the doctors diagnosed the dread disease. In his delirium he several times spoke Nadezhda von Meck's name, reproachfully. He also repeated the phrase, 'I believe it is death', and in St Petersburg at three o'clock in the morning of 6 November it was.

Symphony no. 6 in B Minor (*Pathétique*). In 1891 Tchaikovsky had attempted a sixth symphony, but the result displeased him and in a bout of depression he tore it up. Two years later in a series of letters we come across the following: 'During my travels I had an idea for another symphony . . . I think it is the best of my compositions . . . which I shall certainly not tear up . . . I love it as I've never loved a single one of my other musical progeny.'

The title *Pathétique* was suggested by his brother who tells us, 'I said the word to Peter. "Splendid, bravo!" he cried, and he wrote in my presence the name that will for ever remain.' It has often been presumed that the final movement was Tchaikovsky's foreboding of his own imminent demise.

Piano Concerto no. 1 in B Flat Minor. Tchaikovsky's Christmas Eve in 1874 was an unhappy one indeed. He had just completed but not yet orchestrated his first piano concerto. Eagerly he invited his friend Nikolai Rubinstein, brother of Anton, to listen to it. In a classroom at the Conservatoire, Tchaikovsky played it through, but not a word did Rubinstein utter. At the end, when asked that he thought of it, he let loose a flow of the most vehement condemnation. He declared it to be worthless, vulgar and unplayable. Too pained and angry to speak, Tchaikovsky walked from the room. Presently Rubinstein came to him, for he saw how he'd upset his friend, and said if the concerto were completely revised to suit his requirements he would be glad to play it at his concert. Tchaikovsky refused to change a single note.

When it had been orchestrated a month later, he sent it with a dedication to Hans von Bülow, the eminent pianist and conductor, who replied in the most glowing terms. He found the concerto noble, powerful, distinguished, and gave it its first public performance in Boston that same year to a tremendous reception. One should add that Moscow heard it soon after this for the first time—with Nikolai Rubinstein as the conductor.

Fantasy Overture *Romeo and Juliet*. There is a romantic notion that this overture with its exquisite love music was inspired by Tchaikovsky's infatuation for Désirée Artôt, an opera singer. She encouraged the friendship, for he was a good-looking young man.

Flattered, he devoted all his spare time to her and professed that he loved her with all his heart and soul. But when, within a few months, she had married a Spanish baritone, it didn't appear to break his heart at all. The truth was that the *Romeo and Juliet* theme had been suggested to him by Balakirev when Désirée had been forgotten, and the work was completed a year later. It is the most successful of his early works.

Capriccio Italien. In February 1880 while on a holiday in Rome, Tchaikovsky wrote to Madame von Meck that he had sketched a rough draft of an Italian fantasia based on popular tunes. He told her he thought it had a bright future and would be effective because of the wonderful melodies he happened to have picked up, partly from publishers' collections and partly from some he had heard in the streets. The opening fanfare, for instance, was based on a bugle call which he heard every evening coming from the army barracks near his hotel. He gave the work the new title when he returned to Moscow, where it had its first performance that same year at which it was an outstanding success.

Overture *1812*. This too dates from 1880 when it was introduced at an all-Tchaikovsky concert at the Art and Industrial Exhibition in Moscow. The composer's comments on the piece include his opinion that 'it is not of great artistic value, very noisy . . . only of local and patriotic significance'. It depicts the Russian triumph in defeating the invading Napoleonic armies. The two nations are represented by the Czarist national anthem and the *Marseillaise*, and the work ends on a note of jubilation as the hymn 'God preserve the people' rings out in final victory.

Andante Cantabile is the orchestral arrangement of the attractively wistful slow movement of Tchaikovsky's first String Quartet in D. The main theme is based on a tune he heard a servant whistle

outside his window, a folksong of which the English title is
'Johnny on the sofa'. It is contained in Rimsky-Korsakov's
collection of Russian folk airs.

Swan Lake. Tchaikovsky composed this ballet on a commission
from the Bolshoi Theatre in 1877. He said he undertook it
because he needed the money, and also because he had long
entertained the wish to try his hand at this type of music, having
admired the work of Delibes for many years. A poor performance
and a score above the heads of the public, who were used to trivial
music for dancing, proved its undoing and it was soon taken off.
Tchaikovsky then retrieved some of the best numbers for a
concert suite. The ballet was never again performed in his lifetime, and it was twenty years before *Swan Lake*, with an entirely
new production and new choreography, became the classic it is.

The *Nutcracker* Suite. The ballet is based on a charming fairy-tale
by E. T. A. Hoffman about a little girl, Marie, who dreams after
her Christmas Eve party of a battle in which the nutcracker
defeats the Mouse King who had come with his troops to gobble
all the sweets on the Christmas tree. The nutcracker then turns
into a prince who takes Marie to the land of the Sugar Plum
Fairy, where a series of dances are performed in her honour. The
Nutcracker was first presented with a one-act opera called *Iolanta*,
and both were absolute failures. Before this, however, Tchaikovsky had arranged some of the numbers as a suite and this
enjoyed immediate acclaim; every item was encored. Curiously
the piece of music from the ballet that is the most popular in my
programme is the dramatic *pas de deux*, which is not in the suite.

Widor—Symphony No. 5 in F Minor (*Toccata*)

Apart from this one extremely popular piece, hardly anything is heard of this composer's work today. Charles Marie Widor (1844–1937) was an eminent organist and teacher. In 1869 he became organist at St Sulpice in Paris, a post of some importance which he kept for sixty years. He succeeded César Franck as professor of the organ at the Paris Conservatoire, and had as one of his pupils Albert Schweitzer.

RALPH VAUGHAN WILLIAMS

(1872–1958)

'One of the great men of English music' is how Hubert Foss in his excellent book on the composer refers to him. And he goes on to say: 'The Englishry of Vaughan Williams's music will survive because it comes from the past . . . his nationalism grows from the earth.' Vaughan Williams's interest in folk music was a life-long passion. He believed that the folksong was the great germ from which all musical development ultimately sprang.

He was born in Down Ampney in Gloucestershire, and reported that his first lesson in musical theory was from his aunt, Miss Wedgwood. 'When I was about six I wrote a piano piece four bars long called, heaven knows why, "The Robin's Nest".' His main instrument as a boy was the violin with regard to which he said: 'I believe I should have made quite a decent fiddler but the authorities decided that if I was to take up music at all the violin was too doubtful a career and I must seek safety on the organ stool, a trade for which I was entirely unsuited.' After leaving school—he was at Charterhouse—he went to the Royal College of Music for two years before proceeding to Cambridge, where he took his Bachelor of Music degree. He then returned to the Royal College where he studied under Parry and Stanford. He also went to Berlin for lessons with Max Bruch who, he remembered, encouraged him enormously.

He was thirty-five when *Towards the Unknown Region* was performed with some success at the Leeds Festival. This was the first of his compositions that concert-goers heard. But still feeling that there were yawning gaps in his techniques he took himself off to Paris for some tuition from Ravel, who told him that he was the only pupil who didn't attempt to copy his style. Many years later this comment was answered by Vaughan Williams: 'I couldn't have written Ravel's music if I'd wanted to . . . I am usually content to provide plain cooking, and the proof of the pudding is in the eating.'

Some of the ingredients of his 'plain cooking' he listed for us as long ago as 1912 when, in an article in the Royal College of Music magazine, he wrote: 'Have we not all about us forms of musical expression which we (the British composers) can take and purify and raise to the level of great art? For instance, the lilt of a chorus at a music hall joining in a popular song . . . the rousing fervour of a Salvation Army hymn, St Paul's and a great choir singing in one of its festivals, the Welshmen striking up one of their own hymns whenever they score a goal at an international football match. . . . Have all these nothing to say to us? Have we not in England occasions crying out for music?'

Fantasia on a Theme by Thomas Tallis. Thomas Tallis was one of the most important of sixteenth-century English composers. He was organist of the Chapel Royal and wrote mainly church music, and the theme that Vaughan Williams adapted is one of a set of eight Psalm tunes. The *Fantasia* was first performed in 1909 under the baton of Sir Thomas Beecham, and the following year it was given in Gloucester Cathedral at the Three Choirs Festival.

Fantasia on Greensleeves. Greensleeves is an old English country tune from the sixteenth century. One of the earliest references to it occurs in Shakespeare's play *The Merry Wives of Windsor*. Vaughan Williams wrote the *Fantasia* in 1908 and in 1929 used the melody once again in his opera *Sir John in Love*.

'Linden Lea'. One of the loveliest of Vaughan Williams's songs, the melody is not traditional as many think, but his own, and like so much of his music found its inspiration in the folk tunes of the English countryside. The words of the song are by William Barnes, and come from his 'Poems of Rural Life in Dorset Dialect'.

GIUSEPPE VERDI

(1813–1901)

Verdi's birthplace was the tiny village of Le Roncole in the plain of Lombardy in the north of Italy, where his father was an inn-keeper. When he was four weeks old the world and posterity might have been deprived of one of its musical geniuses. The Russian and Austrian armies had defeated Napoleon and were advancing into Italy. The tiny hamlet lay in the path of the invading forces, who were wreaking havoc as they killed and plundered their way through the countryside. In Le Roncole most of the villagers sought sanctuary in the church. Luigia Verdi, with her infant in her arms, did likewise; but she hastened up into the belfry where she remained terror-stricken while the soldiers below massacred everyone in sight and, having had their fill, departed without looking further.

Verdi's early interest in music was awakened by the strolling musicians who paused at the inn, and by the organ in church. When he was eight he craved to learn music, so his father secured an old spinet, very battered and worn, which was repaired by a village crony called Cavaletti, who lavished all his skill on restoring it. When he returned it there was an inscription inside the lid, detailing the work he had done, without charge because 'the earnestness of the young Verdi in wanting to learn the instrument was sufficient recompense for his work'. And he added the date, 'Anno Domini 1821'. Verdi took lessons from the village organist, and when he was ten was already playing the organ for the church services. His father now thought the boy should have a better education and sent him to school in the nearby town of Busseto. Each Sunday Giuseppe walked the six miles to and from Le Roncole in order to play the organ in church, and for this he received two lire a week. In Busseto he came under the wing of a friend of his father's, Antonio Barezzi, a merchant of standing who was active in the town Philharmonic Society. Barezzi was impressed by the boy's diligence and offered him employment after a time, and the opportunity to further his musical studies with Provesi, the cathedral organist and conductor of the Philharmonic orchestra. Verdi accepted.

He was leading a busy life and his fortunes were changing fast. Within three years he had made such good progress that he frequently deputized for Provesi at the cathedral, conducted the orchestra, and had begun to write his first compositions. These brought him local fame and were thought exceptional enough for a fund to be raised to send him to Milan for more advanced tuition, so at eighteen Verdi set out for Milan in the hope of entering the Conservatoire. But he was rejected. One reason given was that he did not yet possess sufficient musical knowledge.

It was a bitter blow, but he was not discouraged and was advised instead to approach one Lavignia, who was a musician at La Scala and a good teacher. Lavignia thought highly of his pupil and predicted a bright future for him, but after two years Verdi was invited back to Busseto to succeed Provesi who had died. He returned and married Barezzi's daughter, Margherita, who bore him two children while he worked hard at his composition including an opera.

Early in 1839, when his engagements in Busseto came to an end, he took his family and once more moved to Milan with the object of getting his opera produced. In a matter of weeks La Scala accepted it, and in November of that year *Oberto*, the first of Verdi's twenty-eight operas, was presented to the public. *Oberto* did well enough for him to be offered a contract to compose three operas in the next two years. But no sooner had he set to work than the most appalling tragedy befell him. His two children died within a short time of each other, and before the opera, more a comic opera, had been completed, he lost his beloved wife too. Not unexpectedly the work was a failure. Verdi was crushed by the blows that fate had dealt him and had no more desire to continue with music. It was only through the kindly persuasion of Merelli, the impresario of La Scala, who gave him a libretto to read on the subject of Nebuchadnezzar, that Verdi was brought out of his melancholy. Though he several times refused to go back on his resolve not to compose any more, the words of the libretto that he had only casually glanced at kept running through his head. Certain pages had so impressed themselves on him that day by day he came closer to writing the music for it. Eventually in the autumn of 1841 he informed Merelli that *Nabucco* was ready. Its success was undoubted, and it can be regarded as the first contribution to Verdi's lasting fame.

During the next twelve years he composed no less than a dozen operas, including *Ernani*, *Macbeth* and *Luisa Miller*. Then followed what is regarded as his second and finest creative period, beginning with *Rigoletto*, which qualified him to take his place with the greatest of the world's composers. Rossini said: 'In this music I at last recognize Verdi's genius.' *Rigoletto* was the first of a trilogy that consisted also of *Il Trovatore* and *La Traviata*, the latter two appearing in the same year.

From 1859 on music occupied Verdi much less than hitherto. He spent more time at his estate directing the management of his farmlands. He came of peasant stock and remained a man of the soil all his days. It was also in this year that he married Giuseppina Strepponi, a singer he had met twenty years previously and who, from the earliest days of their close friendship, selflessly devoted all her attention to his needs and his care. He became a member of the first Italian parliament. Though his heart was not in politics he stayed a deputy for five years at the insistence of Cavour, whom he admired. Of the music he was now composing two of his finest works came in his old age. He was seventy-four when he created a masterpiece in *Otello*, his first opera for fifteen years, and he was praised as he'd never been before. Then, at the age of eighty, he produced his comic opera *Falstaff*, a remarkable work into which, as the critics said, he had injected the matured wisdom and experience of his whole life.

At the end of 1897 Giuseppina died and Verdi was a broken man. He composed only a little, some of it church music, notably the *Three Sacred Pieces*. But his infirmity was increasing and his days were now numbered. He died in Milan on 27 January 1901, and the whole country mourned him. In Milan the streets were filled as his body was borne to the oratory of the Musicians' Home that he himself had founded for less fortunate members of his profession.

Nabucco. The title is Verdi's own abbreviation of Nabucodonosor, the Italian equivalent of Nebuchadnezzar. It was his first great success, not only musically but also because it reminded the Italian people of their own bitterness under a foreign yoke. They identified themselves with the Hebrew slaves, and the famous chorus has remained an emblem for them. An account of Verdi's funeral tells us: 'Then came one of the great and rare moments when from the soul of the multitude rose out the chorus from *Nabucco* with which Verdi had become the voice of hope for his people sixty years before, "Va pensiero", the song of the enslaved by the Waters of Babylon.'

Rigoletto was written in forty days. Based upon Victor Hugo's drama *Le Roi s'amuse*, it was first given at La Fenice in Venice. Legend has it that Verdi withheld the music of 'La donna è mobile' ('Woman is fickle') until the last moment and even swore the company to secrecy for fear that the tune, which he knew to be a hit, would be heard all over Venice even before the first performance. His suspicion was correct; the aria was encored again and again. The quartet in the same act, 'Bella figlia dell'amore' ('Fairest Daughter of the Graces'), is one of the best examples of concerted music in all opera, and the soprano aria 'Caro Nome' ('Dearest Name') is another among the fine pages in a wonderful score.

Il Trovatore ('The Troubadour'), the second of the great trilogy, was an even bigger success than *Rigoletto*, and is today probably the most popular of all Verdi's operas. It took even less time to write, Verdi having completed the music in twenty-eight days. One writer has referred to it as 'a tragedy that runs the gamut of sorcery, burning at the stake, death by axe, poison and sword'. On this point Verdi remarked: 'Some people say the opera is too sad and there are too many deaths. But in life all is death.' A confused plot is retrieved by magnificent melodies, one of the most familiar being the 'Miserere', chanted by the monks for those about to die, while above it Manrico and Leonora sing their farewell duet. Favourites too are the 'Anvil' Chorus, and the duet in the last scene, 'Ai nostri monti' ('Home to our Mountains').

La Traviata. Adapted from *The Lady of the Camelias* by Dumas, the opera was an utter failure at its first performance and was almost laughed off the stage at one point in the final scene. When the soprano in the role of Violetta, 'the frail one', a lady of enormous proportions, was supposed to be on the point of death from consumption, the audience fell about. Apart from that, many considered the opera immoral. When it was introduced to London three years later *The Times* railed at 'the representation of all that is foul and hideous in human nature'. But as Verdi himself said after the first night: 'Was the fault mine or the singers'? Time will tell.' The years have given their answer. The Preludes to Act I and Act III, the drinking song 'Libiamo', 'di Provenza il mar' and 'Addio del passato' are just some of the opera's musical delights.

Aida. This opera was commissioned by the Khedive of Egypt for the Italian opera house in Cairo, and had its first performance there in 1871. *Aida* is surely the finest entertainment in the fullest sense that Verdi ever conceived. Its setting in Egypt at the time of the Pharaohs gives it all the appeal of a great pageant, and the finale to the second act is a most spectacular showpiece, both musically and scenically. Six weeks after its Cairo première it was presented at La Scala, Milan, with Verdi conducting. Kobbé wrote that 'he was recalled thirty-two times and presented with an ivory baton and diamond star with the name of *Aida* in rubies, and his own in other precious stones'. Some of the opera's many memorable moments include the tenor aria 'celeste Aida', the Grand March, Aida's aria 'Ritorna vincitor' (victorious return), and the final tragic duet 'o terra addio' ('Farewell, O Earth, Farewell thou vale of sorrow').

RICHARD WAGNER
(1813–1883)

It is only natural that opinions about music should differ as much as they do about anything else. But Wagner's case is an exceptional one. Whether his music repels or enchants us, or whether, like Rossini, we think that 'Wagner's work contains some fine moments but some bad quarters of an hour'; whether we listen to his music simply as music or try to understand and fathom its inner depths, there can be no question that he was unique. No man in the whole history of musical art has been so reviled for what he was and so idolized for what he achieved. His music has been condemned as 'corrupting', 'poisonous' and 'degenerate'. And yet on the other hand his genius was such that he was called 'the greatest man who ever existed'. Hans von Bülow, whose wife Wagner stole, even afterwards spoke of 'this glorious unique man whom one must venerate like a god'.

Deems Taylor in his essay on Wagner calls him 'a monster'. 'He was arrogant, conceited. Other men's money and other men's wives he took without a scruple . . . he could be callous and heartless to a degree that would have made a Roman emperor shudder.' Every line of this essay points to a Wagner imperfection, a sin, a twist of mind, and yet this is how Taylor continues: 'Everything that I have said about him you can find on record. In newspapers, in police reports, in the testimony of people who knew him . . . but the curious thing about this record is that it doesn't matter in the least. . . . When you consider that he wrote thirteen operas and music dramas, eleven of them still holding the stage and eight of them unquestionably worth ranking among the world's great music-drama masterpieces—when you listen to what he wrote, then the debts and heartaches that people had to endure from him don't seem much of a price. . . .'

Richard was the ninth child in the Wagner household in Leipzig. His early interest was literature, and music held little attraction for him until he was fourteen he and heard a Beethoven symphony for the first time. Remarking on it in later years he said: 'I thereupon fell ill and when I awoke I was a musician.' He had had a few piano lessons and even at this age his views clashed with his teacher's. They parted company, and he continued his musical education on his own, poring over Beethoven scores as a labour of love. When he was seventeen an overture of his was performed at a local theatre. He had already started to experiment, which perhaps was why the audience was bewildered. Except for six months' tuition with the cantor of St Thomas's School, from whom he learned a great deal, he developed his talents by his own efforts. He was more fortunate three years later when his (first) symphony received a performance in Prague and at Leipzig's famous concert hall, the Gewandhaus.

At this time, through his brother Albert who was a singer and stage manager at a wretched little theatre in Würzburg, he was engaged as chorus master at what was then the equivalent of a pound a month. When he left there he moved from one small provincial theatre to another conducting dreadful little bands and leading a thoroughly miserable existence. Embittered and disillusioned, he knew he was worthy of better things. He was constantly heavily in debt and harassed by his creditors. Added to which he took himself a wife, a marriage he soon regretted. In 1839, after two years in Riga, his debts had so mounted, and the harassment become so considerable, that he was told it was no longer safe for him to remain, and he and his wife had to flee the country and cross the frontier by way of a smugglers' route.

He now decided to make for Paris. While he was in Riga he had begun to work on his opera *Rienzi* and he had with him in his luggage the partially completed manuscript with which he was going to take Paris by storm.

Arriving in Boulogne Wagner was able to meet Meyerbeer, the opera composer whom he much admired and who happened to be staying in the town. He impressed Meyerbeer sufficiently to be given letters of introduction to various important people connected with opera in Paris. During the time he was putting the finishing touches to *Rienzi* he took any kind of hack work that was available, but he was in desperate straits and was twice imprisoned for debt. All efforts to get *Rienzi* performed failed. Paris would have none of him. Instead he sent it to Dresden, where it was immediately accepted. Encouraged by this, he completed *The Flying Dutchman* within five months.

Again the Royal Opera at Dresden was pleased to receive his work. Wagner had now won a reputation, and he was offered the position of principal conductor there. During the six years he occupied the post, *Tannhäuser* was also performed, and by 1848 *Lohengrin* was ready for production too. But Wagner's involvement in the revolution that year brought him under the suspicion of the authorities and he was forced to escape. When he reached Weimar he got news that a warrant was out for his arrest, and Liszt, who had befriended him, was able to get him to Switzerland in safety, where he remained in exile for twelve years.

It was during this period that he devoted his energies to writing numerous books and pamphlets which expounded his theories about opera. He called for a rejection of the old traditions and formulated his ideas of the music-drama which were to culminate in the colossal achievement of his life, *The Ring of the Nibelung*.

The Ring comprises four music-dramas, *Das Rheingold* ('The Rhinegold'), *Die Walküre* ('The Valkyrie'), *Siegfried* and *Götterdämmerung* ('The Twilight of the Gods'). They form a continuous story based on German legends, and the librettos for the operas were his own work too. This was altogether an achievement which has been described as 'the noblest and greatest work ever attempted by the creative mind'.

After his return to Germany he moved to Bayreuth where, through the enthusiasm of his admirers all over the world and the money they subscribed, he was able to bring to fruition his dream of an ideal theatre for the purpose of staging his music-dramas as he visualized them. In August 1876 the theatre opened with the first complete performance of the *Ring* cycle. With the presentation of *Parsifal* in 1882 his triumph was complete. Yet little more than half a year later, in Venice, he was taken suddenly ill and the end followed quickly.

Tannhäuser. This contains some of Wagner's most popular music. The overture, long a favourite in the concert hall, is a condensed statement of the whole opera. A fanfare of trumpets heralds the stately procession of the guests who have come to witness the song contest. They enter to the strains of the *Grand March*. At the beginning of the third act comes the *Pilgrims' Chorus*, their chant rising from the valley, With their gradual approach the music swells to a superb crescendo, and then fades as it came. Following this, in the half-light of evening, Wolfram, the minstrel knight, accompanying himself on his lyre, sings the beautiful 'O Star of Eve'.

The Ride of the Valkyries. The third act of *Die Walküre* opens with this, one of the most famous of Wagner's orchestral pieces for which he himself prepared a concert version. The scene is the wild mountain-top retreat of the Valkyries, the nine warrior sisters and daughters of Wotan. The music describes their flight through the air as they spur their winged steeds on and on, their wild cries penetrating the roar of the tempest, their armour gleaming in the flashes of lightning that rend the wind-driven storm clouds, each of them carrying the body of a hero slain in battle tied to her saddle.

The Siegfried Idyll. Early on Christmas morning in 1870, Wagner's wife Cosima was awakened by the sounds of music flooding the house. Curious to discover whence it came, she left her room and saw grouped on the staircase a small orchestra with her husband at their head conducting. The serenade was his birthday present to her, and a token of his gratitude for the birth of their son Siegfried. He had composed it in secrecy and rehearsed it the evening before at a hostelry near by.

Tristan und Isolde (Liebestod). The opera is generally conceded to have been inspired by Wagner's own love for Mathilde Wesendonck, the legacy of 'the fairest of all his dreams'. Nowhere else can one find music of such beauty as is set to this tragic love story. *Liebestod* ('Love in Death') is one of the composer's highest achievements, the scene in which Isolde pours out her lament over the dead body of Tristan before she herself falls dying. In concerts the love music is usually joined with the Prelude to form a perfect summary of the opera's tragic elements.

'The Warsaw Concerto'

This piece for piano and orchestra became a great favourite during World War II and has held its popularity ever since. It was composed by Richard Addinsell for the film *Dangerous Moonlight*. Addinsell (born 1904) read law at Oxford before going to the Royal College of Music. He has written Hollywood film scores and was also well known as a theatre composer.

CARL MARIA WEBER
(1786–1826)

Carl Maria was a sick child from birth, but his father's part in his upbringing was not calculated to improve his condition. Weber senior was something of a reprobate. He was German, a musician of sorts and a strolling player who had never had the mind to settle. When he was fifty he married a girl of sixteen, and Carl Maria was their first born. Perhaps to compensate for his own failures, and having been fired by tales of the glory and, as he thought, wealth that had been accorded the young Mozart, he had dreams of producing an infant prodigy of his own. The two sons of his previous marriage had disappointed him in this, and he was now determined to realize his ambition with Carl Maria. The boy's musical education was started at a very early age, but as his father moved from place to place so did he move from teacher to teacher. Nevertheless, by the age of nine he was composing with facility, and through his father's close contact with the theatre, his first youthful experience of the stage and its workings had made a deep impression on him and stimulated an interest in the theatre that was to influence his future path.

He was barely fourteen when his first opera was presented, and though it met with no marked favour he pressed on, and two years later another of his works came before the public. He was already showing signs of great talent, and was still only seventeen when he was appointed musical director at Breslau. It may well have been that the responsibility of directing a theatre and conducting an orchestra, in both of which capacities he was more than able, proved too much for him, and he resorted to dissipation, moving in bad company and landing himself with substantial debts. Moreover, an accident in drinking nitric acid in mistake for wine nearly cost him his life and ended his term at Breslau.

In 1810 further disaster struck him when his father appeared on the scene; he had apparently stolen some money from his son's bureau that had belonged to somebody else. While Carl Maria was in the theatre rehearsing a new opera the police arrived and took him off to prison. Though his innocence was established, he and his father were conducted to the frontier and expelled. It is interesting at this point to note what Weber wrote in his diary when his father died: 'It is beyond measure painful to me that I could do no more to promote his happiness. May God bless him for all the great love he bore me which I did not deserve, and for the education he bestowed upon me.' The unfortunate episode had a moderating effect on him and he began to work harder than ever. Two operas were produced in quick succession, and a large number of other compositions, including a piano concerto, were the result of his activity at this time.

But he was still unsettled and a wanderer. He spoke of himself as 'weighed down by the struggle against adverse circumstances'. His luck changed to some extent when he went to Prague to reorganize the once famous theatre, now neglected, where Mozart had first presented *Don Giovanni*. Weber devoted all his energies to reviving its former glory, and the success of the enterprise secured for him the post of musical director at Dresden. Here he set himself the task of creating a German opera in its true sense, casting off the Italian influence that had for so long dominated the stage. In 1821 he was to achieve his object with his own work, *Der Freischütz*, but owing to the prejudice that still existed in Dresden it was brought out in Berlin where it was proclaimed a masterpiece. It was the beginning of a new tradition in the opera houses of Germany.

Der Freischütz was presented all over Europe to tremendous ovations. In London it was a sensation. So highly was Weber now thought of that he received a commission from Covent Garden for a new opera. The chosen subject was Oberon, and he worked on it for a year, taking English lessons at the same time so that he could better supervise the production. Though he was a very sick man he insisted on going to London in the face of his physicians' advice to attend the rehearsals and conduct the twelve performances for which he was contracted. He probably knew he hadn't long to live but he needed the money he would make from this engagement and concerts to provide for his family in this eventuality. After the first performance he wrote to his wife that he'd never met with such success. 'When I entered the orchestra the whole house rose as of one accord, and an incredible applause, cheers, waving of hats and handkerchiefs received me and was hardly to be quieted.'

Two months later Weber was dead. He was too broken in health to stand the strain and excitement. He was buried in Moorfields, but in 1844 the coffin was removed and borne with great ceremony to his native country.

Much of Weber's music is not as frequently heard as it should be. In my programme I have played the *Konzertstück*, the first clarinet concerto and various other works, but the public know him best by his *Invitation to the Dance*. This is perhaps his most important piano work and introduced a pattern to be followed later by such waltz composers as Strauss and Waldteufel. Weber called it a 'Rondo brilliant'. But today it is popular only in the orchestration made by Berlioz in 1841 for a performance of *Der Freischütz* at the Paris Opéra. It was the inspiration too for Diaghilev's ballet *Le Spectre de la Rose*.

Overture to *Oberon*. The overture was the last part of the opera to be completed, a month after rehearsals had started in London. On the manuscript Weber added the words 'Finished April 9th 1826 in the morning at a quarter of twelve and with it the whole opera. Soli Dei Gloria [Glory be to God Alone] C. M. Weber.'

POSTLUDE

A little while ago I ventured upon this remark: 'In a world where everything seems to come out desperately wrong, good music comes out exquisitely right.' A viewpoint with which we can all agree. It is my hope that the foregoing notes will add a further interest to that music and, if only in a small way, act as a companion to your future listening. I have endeavoured to do no more than present in an undemanding fashion those brief details about the composers and their music that preface the records I play on Sunday evenings. Wherever possible it has been my intention to avoid the language of the dry reference book, while attempting at the same time to give the creators of the music a modicum of flesh and blood. I trust I have succeeded in this. I am aware that I have omitted some composers and much music that my listeners would no doubt like to have seen included, but the sphere is vast and my space limited.

As you will have noticed, there are in this collection many more than just the hundred tunes that headed the last poll. As tastes change, and they are bound to, and more and more lesser known music is introduced to the programme, it would be interesting to speculate on which of the present pieces would lose their position in any further vote, and which would replace them. My experience has shown me that listeners are, on the whole, constant in their allegiance to the music they have learned to love.

Only in one or two instances have I specifically mentioned gramophone records; I have refrained from advising particular performances as their availability is not always certain. Listeners would do well to keep in touch with current releases as once-deleted records are regularly being reissued, very often in bargain issues.

Finally, I should like to say that I have enjoyed compiling this book, and I hope that you will derive as much pleasure as you dip into it from time to time.

INDEX